The
PONDERING
POLE 2

Ed Poniewaz

2020–2023 and "Best Of"

The Pondering Pole 2
2020–2023 and "Best Of"

© 2023 by Ed Poniewaz

ISBN: 978-1-63110-558-6

All Rights Reserved Under
International and Pan-American Copyright Conventions.
No part of this book may be used or reproduced in any manner whatsoever without written permission except in the case of brief quotations embodied in critical articles or reviews.

Cover Photos by Sue Poniewaz

Tee Shirt worn by Ed Poniewaz on the front cover
designed by Katheryne Morschl

Printed in the United States of America by
Graphic Connections Group Publishing
Chesterfield, Missouri 63005

Contents

Section I. Introduction 1

Section II. 2020 5
    January 2020 **Is Nationalism a Dirty Word?**. 7
    February 2020 **Ewelina i Ewelina**. 10
    March 2020 **And now, he-e-e-e-r-r-e-e-'s Jenny!** 13
    April 2020 **Beautiful things**. 16
    May-June 2020 **May is the month for feminism**. 19
    July-August 2020 **Monuments and Makowiec**. 22
    September 2020 **"Just another day on the job."**. 25
    November 2020 **A 1496 Project?**. 29
    December 2020 **Warsaw Cool**. 32

Section III. 2021 35
    January 2021 **1. d4 d5 2. c4** 37
    February 2021 **Father Dzierozynski: a worthy life**. 39
    March 2021 **A rule to live by**. 43
    April 2021 **The four P's**. 46
    May-June 2021 **"One of the great poems of the world."** 50
    July-August 2021 **"King of the Burin."**. 53
    September 2021 **About sausage "the way they used to" make it**. . . 57
    October 2021 **Saving all the "towns," "hills," and "villages."** 61
    November 2021 **Anything you can do…** 64
    December 2021 **"I owe everything to America."** 67

Section IV. 2022 71

    January 2022 ~~Star Trek~~ Polonia: The next generation. 73

    February 2022 **Lodz you believe it.** 77

    March 2022 **Trains, Planes, and… Well, just trains.** 80

    April 2022 **From lab rat to CEO.** 84

    May-June 2022 **In pursuit of a cure..** 87

    July-August 2022 **MAUS no more?.** 91

    September 2022 **Modern Polish church music.** 94

    October 2022 **Breaking and making bread..** 98

    November 2022 **Legendary hurricanes and their trackers..** 100

Section V. 2023 103

    January 2023 **The love of all things that are…** 105

    February 2023 **"And the winner is… ".** 108

    March 2023 **Changing the historical narrative..** 112

    April 2023 **And He will raise you up.** 117

Section VI. 2013 123

    January 2013 **Milestones.** 125

    March 2013 **Farewell to the "Perfect Knight."** 128

    April 2013 **Linkage.** 130

    May 2013 **"The Eagle Unbowed.".** 133

    August 2013 **"Making" Tamales and Golabkis.** 136

    September 2013 **You go Oprah!** 138

    October 2013 **A Tribute to the Polka Club.** 141

    December 2013 **What was all the pondering about?** 144

Section VII. 2014 147

    January 2014 **So now what?** 149

    April 2014 **Lenten meditation.** 153

    June 2014 ***Delivery Man***, **DreamWorks SKG**
        and Touchstone Pictures, 2013. 155

    September 2014 **An idea..** 157

    October 2014 **Maestro..** 159

    November 2014 **There was a time....** 162

    December 2014 **Talki Polski** .165

Section VIII. 2015... 169

    January 2015 **Achievers and Greasers.** 171

    February 2015 **Lasso the moon!** 175

    March 2015 **Spring, at last.** .178

    April 2015 **Office of the Mayor.** 181

    May 2015 **Shout out to the polka snowbirds of Daytona.** 184

    June 2015 **This is cool..** 186

    July 2015 **A family affair.** 188

    August 2015 **Al's Little League.** 191

    October 2015 **Son of Poland, Son of East St. Louis.** 193

    December 2015 PAJ **Wise Children from the East.** 195

Section IX. Dziekuje Bardzo!... 199

I
Introduction

Przybieżeli do Betlejem pasterze, Grając skocznie Dzieciąteczku na lirze.
Refrain: Chwała na wysokości, chwała na wysokości, A pokój na ziemi.

Oddawali swe ukłony w pokorze, Tobie z serca ochotnego, o Boże! - Refrain

Lulajże Jezuniu moja perełko, Lulajże Jezuniu me pieścidełko!
Refrain: Lulajże Jezuniu, lulajże, lulaj, A Ty Go Matuchno w płaczu utulaj.

Zamknijże znużone płaczem powieczki, Utulże zemdlone kwileniem usteczki. - Refrain

Pójdźmy wszyscy do stajenki; Do Jezusa i Panienki;
Refrain: Powitajmy Maleńkiego, I Maryję, Matkę Jego.

Witaj Jezu ukochany, Od Patriarchów czekany,
Od Proroków ogłoszony, Od narodów upragniony. - Refrain

Cicha noc, Święta noc. Wszystko śpi, atoli, Czuwa Józef i Maryja.
Niech więc Bożka ich Dziecina W błogim pokoju śpi, W błogim pokoju śpi.

Silent night, holy night! All is calm, all is bright. 'Round young Virgin Mother and Child,
Holy Infant so tender and mild, Sleep in heavenly peace; Sleep in heavenly peace.

*T*his is the second installment of *The Pondering Pole*. For those not familiar with *The Pondering Pole*, here is my story.

> *Over fifteen years ago I discovered the Polish American Journal published out of Buffalo, New York. I was very impressed with this monthly newspaper for Polish Americans and approached the editor with an idea for a column that would be about famous, successful, or important Americans or others that have a Polish background or connection but were not familiar or even known to Poles or non-Poles, either because they lived under a changed name, or their importance was not apparent or well known. He thought the idea was a good one and gave me the name for the column:* **The Pondering Pole.**

My goal with every Pondering Pole column (and I continue to write them) is still the same: to educate the reader and give them something uplifting, positive, and interesting about Polish. Identifying important, interesting, or successful persons, places, or events that have a Polish connection is a way to give those in and outside the Polish community this information.

The format of the column is to first highlight and present the subject in the body of the column, and then mention or ask in the following section whether another person or persons or subject had a Polish background or connection called "Polish or Not?" Most recently the title for this section has been changed to "DNA Diary," mainly because in some cases I already note that the person or thing is in fact Polish.

The final paragraph usually closes with a mention of the monthly Polish or American holiday or current event, sometimes a one or two sentence recap of the main topic, and then a thank you to anyone that contributed to the column. Lastly, I always ask, if "you have a thought about this month's topic, have a question, or have interesting facts to share" please write or eMail me. I'm still always open to receiving research and knowledge from the readers where there is a question about someone's or something's ethnicity, so please share. When I do get a response, it is encouraging. It is wonderful to engage the reader, good or bad.

I began writing *The Pondering Pole* in 2005 and the first Pondering Pole book was a compilation of articles from the years 2016 through 2019. This edition begins with the year 2020 through 2022 and into 2023. The second Pondering Pole follows nicely from the first book and because 2020 and 2021 were the "COVID" years, the events and people from that period were many times a great source of inspiration. Also included are some "Best Of" columns and parts of columns from years prior to 2016 that I hope you will enjoy.

Besides the goal of the Pondering Pole to educate the reader with something uplifting, positive, and interesting about being Polish, it was also a selfish way for me to understand my ethnicity, shape my life, and help me understand other cultures. Culture comparison is a good thing and rather than grade one against the other, it makes for a more healthy and grounded perspective of other people, their history, and their culture. It has been a wonderful experience and adventure. I recommend you do the same in whatever form suits you best.

Please note that some of the references to people, places, and events have changed since the creation of this book. Some of the places no longer exist and some of the events are no longer scheduled. That is life in an ethnic community as places, traditions, rituals, and gatherings change. Life changes. Some of the articles that originally appeared in the Polish American Journal have been updated, or left out, mainly for space considerations, and have been cleaned up to make for easier reading.

I hope you enjoy *The Pondering Pole 2 2020-2023 and "Best Of"*.

II
2020

January 2020

Is Nationalism a Dirty Word?

*F*irst there were tribes, then princedoms, then kingdoms, then nations. The people of the nation feel a connection and an allegiance to an area or land governed by law and a leader. When there is a lasting and strong connection then Nationalism becomes more apparent and prominent. Some do not like the nationalist or patriotic spirit because it can be exclusionary or aggressive; others are ambivalent or unaffected by it.

Poles are typically seen as having a nationalist character and those from the outside often interpret it negatively. That view of Nationalism historically was linked to anti-Semitism and more recently it is described as xenophobia or as an anti-Western bias. I remember watching a documentary where the narrator described Poland as "one of the most nationalistic countries in Europe" prior to the start of World War II with the implication not only would the nation proudly resist invasion by the Nazis but also that Polish-Jewish relations leading up to the war were harmed by this Nationalism. Perhaps Poland's nationalist spirit has engendered some counter-productive behavior but on balance I believe it has been a force for the well-being and survival of the nation.

There is an online article with a positive spin on that subject as it relates to Poland and many of the countries in Eastern Europe. The article is *Economic Nationalism Made Eastern Europe More Resilient* by Leonid Bershidsky (https://www.yahoo.com/finance/news/economic-nationalism-made-eastern-europe-130633415.html). The point of the piece is how fluctuations in the business cycles in Germany affect the economies of countries like Poland, Czech Republic, and Hungary because of their close relationship with their large and powerful German neighbor. This "dependence" on the German economy has prompted observers to peg Poland and others as "colonies" or subjects of the German Republic.

As Bershidsky points out though, Poland, Hungary, and the Czech Republic especially have withstood downturns in German economic cycles because they have instituted "expansionary fiscal policies" and they have employed a "conscious strategy of export diversification." From the article:

> *... Hungary and Poland have also reduced their export dependence on Germany by 10 percentage points and 7 percentage points respectively during the same period but they've done more than just weaning themselves off Europe's biggest economy. Poland, for instance, now produces more finished products than intermediate goods such as parts, which wasn't the case at the turn of the century.*

This is great news and although relations with their mighty neighbor are amiable, prudent, and reasonable, I do hope they shake off the grip Germany has on the many aspects of national sovereignty that would smell of dominance. It will be refreshing to realize that these Eastern European peoples are finally emerging as truly independent and resourceful nations. Even if that movement concerned solely with the economy is called Nationalism, then so be it. Please read the article to get the full story.

Polish or Not?

Izabella Miko is a Polish born actress who has worked in television and film for thirty years. She is listed as an actress, dancer, producer, and environmental activist. Born Izabella Anna Mikolajczak, January 21, 1981, in Lodz, Poland, Izabella began her career in the arts as a ballet dancer and after an injury moved more into acting. While already established in Poland's film industry, her big break came in the United States when she received a part in the movie *Coyote Ugly* and then followed up with a starring role in the film *The Forsaken*.

She has appeared in recurring roles for the television shows *Deadwood* and *Chicago Fire*. Recent endeavors include a part as Cassie in the 2018 movie *The Rake* and as Helen Hirsch in the television series *The Hunt*. Beauty, talent, and a woman working between two universes, Pollywood and Hollywood, Izabella Miko.

In the movie *The Grand Budapest Hotel*, the setting is a fictional country called "Zubrowka." Zubrowka as we know is a special Polish vodka. The name used in *Grand Budapest* is supposed to be facetious, quaint, or perhaps (but hopefully not), satirical. If you know why "Zubrowka" was chosen for the movie, let me know.

So, there is a new 3D computer-animated movie now playing called *The Addams Family* which is a sequel to the original *The Addams Family* film released in 1991. A theme that runs throughout is the character Pugsley's "Mazurka," a "rite of passage that every Addams family member takes."

Is this Mazurka also facetious, quaint, or satirical? Perhaps the writer used the same inspiration and motive that was employed in *Grand Budapest,* and we hope this it is also a harmless one. I happen to love the unusual nature (by Western standards) of the Polish words and names. In fact, I once suggested to my artist daughter to do a whole series of prints with variations on just the name/word *Poniewaz*. There are other spectacular names of course.

A new CEO for McDonald's!! Chris Kempczinski is now running the great American hamburger company. Chris grew up in Cincinnati, Ohio, his dad, Richard Kempczinski was an associate professor of surgery and chief of vascular surgery at the University of Cincinnati Medical Center, mom was a kindergarten teacher, and thus he became a graduate of Duke University and the Harvard Business School. Good genes beget good genes.

Before McDonald's, Kempczinski held management positions at Procter & Gamble, PepsiCo, and Kraft Foods. We wish him well and all success in his new position, and although he has a Polish name, we still need to ask, is Chris, Polish or not?

February 2020

Ewelina i Ewelina.

How about Ewelina for a Polish girl's name? It can be Anglicized to Evalina or Evalena, Eve or Eva for short, and Evie or Lina as a nickname. Or, crazy I know, just leave it the way it is spelled in Polish. This is a tale of two Ewelinas.

The Pondering Pole is often described as featuring "interesting and *successful* people, places, and events that have a Polish connection." Successful is an appropriate description when winning the 2019 Smithsonian American Ingenuity Awards for Life Sciences. Dr. Ewelina Mamcarz along with Dr. Stephen Gottschalk are the recipients of this honor for developing a treatment for babies born without an immune system. Kids with this kind of biological deficiency are typically described as having the "bubble boy disease."

Doctor Mamcarz was born in Poland and received her degree at the Medical University of Silesia (Slaska Akademia Medyczna) in Katowice, Poland. She is a fellow in the Bone Marrow Transplant Department at St. Jude Research Hospital in Memphis, Tennessee, and led the clinical trial for this project. She has a number of publications on this and other topics and is extremely optimistic about the results so far. In an interview for BioSpace website (https://www.biospace.com/article/st-jude-s-gene-therapy-appears-to-cure-bubble-boy-disease), she stated,

> *All of these patients were able to come off of isolation and they've returned home with immune systems that were fully functional. We had patients come to us with very severe infections and they cleared them through the emergence of this newly developed immune system... They are home, some have started daycare, and they are making antibodies in response to vaccines just like we all do.*

Congratulations to Dr. Ewelina Mamcarz for her splendid work in this key area of medical research and for her contributions to making our health and wellbeing better.

Searching for Ewelina Mamcarz in Wikipedia popped up several other Ewelinas and this one especially intrigued me. I have never read anything by the novelist Honoré de Balzac, a famous and influential French writer in the first half of the 1800s, but his relationship and later love affair with Ewelina Hanska is super interesting.

Ewelina Rzewuska was a rich Polish woman of noble birth who married Waclaw Hanski, also a Pole, who was also extraordinarily rich and a nobleman, more as a strategic arrangement rather than out of love. Hanski's estate comprised 21,000 acres near the city of Wierzchownia in the Russian partitioned Kiev Governate in Ukraine. Already possessing an interest in literature and philosophy, Ewelina read and became infatuated with the writings of de Balzac and in 1832, she wrote an anonymous letter expressing admiration for him and praising his writing. "In 1833, they met for the first time, in Switzerland. Soon afterward he began writing the novel *Seraphita*, which includes a character based on Hanska." Their relationship continued and then in 1841, Waclaw Hanski, twenty years older than Ewelina, passed away.

The association between Balzac and Hanska began with inspiration and eventually progressed to collaboration. At least one expert has maintained that his "greatness" only began after his relationship with Hanska and is seen in a number of his works:

> *She can be seen as the model for La Fosseue, Mme Claes, Modesta Mignon, Ursule Mirouet, Adelina Houlot, and especially Eugenie Grandet and Mme de Mortsauf. There is less agreement among scholars on whether she was also the inspiration for more negative characters such as Fedora and Lady Dudley, as Balzac seems to have used her mostly as a model for more positive personas. His works also mention numerous characters named Eve or Eveline and have several dedications to her.*

In 1850 Ewelina Hanska and Honore de Balzac married and moved to Paris where they lived until his death in 1860. Power comes in many forms but the power that Ewelina Hanska had with Honore de Balzac was immense.

THE PONDERING POLE 2   2020–2023 and "BEST OF"

Theirs was a great love story that sparked unforgettable literary prose and characters.

This might be farfetched, but based on what I know now, Balzac is as much (at least indirectly) for the Poles as he is for the French, and this is something I am curious to explore and confirm. If you have already explored it, please share your thoughts.

Polish or Not?

Remember the actress, Joan Blondell? A beautiful and sexy woman, she starred in films during the 30s, 40s, and 50s but stayed around into the 1980s and did some TV as well. The Turner Classic Movie channel had a 24-hour run of her movies in December. Here is her Polish connection from Wikipedia:

Rose Joan Blondell was born in New York to a vaudeville family… Her father, Levi Bluestein, a vaudeville comedian known as Ed Blondell, was born in Poland to a Jewish family in 1866.

There is a company called Carpe (https://www.mycarpe.com) that makes a variety of products but the ad I saw features a lotion for people with sweaty hands. CEO and co-founder David Spratte along with COO and co-founder Kasper Kubica appear in the ad. I wish these guys all the success in the world. Kubica sounds like a very Polish name but is COO and co-founder Kasper Kubica, Polish, or not?

March 2020

And now, he-e-e-e-r-r-e-e-'s Jenny!

*T*he typical Polish personality is more on the reserved side, quiet, contemplative, but fun loving and possessing a dry sense of humor. I want to introduce you to a person with all that and more. Her name is Jenny Milkowski, known also as "Jenny Milk" or "JMilk" and she is a host, reporter, and weather and traffic anchor on CBS Channel 8 in San Diego, California. She is a Polish girl with bardzo personality! Check out her website (https://www.jennymilkowski.com) and you can find other examples of her work as a TV personality on YouTube. You will see lots of big, enthusiastic, "I love life" smiles and I love that.

In examining Jenny's life, a couple of things stand out. First, she is a very hard worker with a lot of determination to succeed, and second, she possesses an inner confidence, drive, and strength that says, American, *and Polish*, is who I am and if you have a problem with it, sorry, but I am going to keep being me. Let me show you what I am talking about.

Jenny Milk is a graduate of the University of Illinois at Urbana-Champaign with a B.S. in broadcast journalism. She was a member of The Second City Chicago comedy troupe and the Acting Studio in Chicago. Her broadcasting career began at WJFW Newswatch, Channel 12 in 2006 in Rhinelander, Wisconsin, as a reporter and weekend weather producer and anchor. Like many of the great ones, she began at a small station with high hopes.

WJFW Newswatch started her on the path to all things media. After a stint with NBC Universal in 2007 as a production assistant, she got on with the Tribune Company and was a news producer and *ChicagoNow* blogger for the next five years. In 2012 she was employed by CBS where she won an Emmy Award for her writing and producing. Jenny became a co-owner of MUU MEDIA LLC and was nominated for another Emmy while working as a traffic reporter for Total Traffic Network in Chicago. From March 2018 to when she transferred to the CBS affiliate in San Diego, she was a host of the "Jenny Milk & Jay" show at Hubbard Broadcasting in Chicago. Jenny

Milkowski has "been around" in her career in radio and television but it has been a very impressive journey.

Part of the reason for her success is because she is secure in her Polish skin. Per her website, both parents are Polish immigrants; she embraces that ethnicity, and even flaunts it. She is not shy to say that Polish was her first language as a child and being crowned queen of the Pierogi Fest in Whiting, Illinois was a big deal for her. An article from the Crazy Polish Guy website (https://crazypolishguy.com) puts it all into perspective from her days broadcasting in Chicago.

> *Jenny brings a uniquely Polish personality to the weekday morning show at FOX-TV Chicago, "Good Day Chicago." Aside from sprinkling informational tidbits about Poland in between her traffic reports, she serves as an on-air Polish guru. That's right. Whenever anyone at the station is covering anything involving Polish culture, you can probably bet that Jenny will be involved. Her Polish pride shines through the TV camera lens, making her among the most passionate and visible proponents of Polish culture in the Chicago metropolitan area.*

Wouldn't you love to sit down to dinner with Jenny Milk, not only to hear about her experiences in the news world, but all her thoughts on growing up Polish in the United States of America and growing up Polish in the United States of "the media?" I am thinking at least one bottle of vodka and maybe two.

Polish or Not?

"Lionel the Lion Faced Man." His real name was Stephan Bibrowski, born in 1890 in a town called Bielsk in Congress Poland and he died in 1932. Stephen was born with long hair that covered his entire body in a horrible way and he was given up by his family as a young child. Eventually Bibrowski found employment as a circus sideshow performer. His condition was probably hypertrichosis (excessive growth of hair). Other sideshow performers you might know are Chang and Eng, "The Original Siamese Twins," Zip, "The Pinhead," Joseph Merrick, "The Elephant Man," and "General Tom Thumb," the world's smallest man.

Many of the performers had talents that went along with or beyond their peculiar features or looks. Their fates were mixed with some becoming worldly popular and others descending to the lowest rung of ridicule and outcast in society. Though it seems like the Poles have operated on the periphery of human history, in this camp Stephen Bibrowski fit in quite nicely. For him and the rest of "freaks" of the circus, we can only feel sympathy for their condition and their lives. God bless "Lionel the Lion Faced Man."

April 2020

Beautiful things.

When your two-year old grandson reaches out his hand and says, "come here Dziadzia," even in a garbled baby way, well, that makes it all worth it. Sometimes he just says, "Dziage" (rhymes with mirage) and that works too. For two-year old Frankie and my other grandkids, I will always be Dziadzia and I hope they always call me Dziadzia. My hope is that you Polish guys out there also become a Dziadzia someday. Or even just Dziage. It truly is a beautiful thing.

Speaking of beautiful things, I was surprised to find an article in Wikipedia on the "Polish Cathedral Architectural Style" in the United States, something I would not consider as a subject unto itself or even as a category of study, type, or, as in this case, style. There are a lot of beautiful and large immigrant churches in the United States, and many can be thought of as cathedral-like, but I am thrilled by the concept and uniqueness of this one about us.

Wiki defines the Polish Cathedral style as a "North American genre of Catholic church architecture found throughout the Great Lakes and Middle Atlantic regions as well as in parts of New England." Though not technically cathedrals with seats for the bishop in the diocese, for most Poles, the idea is that they functioned as their own "seat" or at the least a center of national and spiritual prominence in the city, the town, or the neighborhood in which they lived.

The main characteristics of the Polish Cathedral are a grand stature and "large amounts of ornamentation in the exterior and interior." The structural form has been described as Eclecticism which incorporates different forms such as Renaissance, Romanesque revival, Baroque, and neo-classical. Those I have seen have exteriors which tend to have a Greco-Roman façade, in the shape of a Greek cross with Roman arched windows and one or more large towers on each side. There are one or more domes inside, a cruciform layout (in the shape of a cross), and stained-glass windows throughout.

The Wiki article lists many of these Polish Cathedrals throughout the United States and I would encourage you to see the list and even visit as many as possible. If visiting St. Louis, Missouri, be sure to see St. Stanislaus Kostka, which I would say is a perfectly designed church in the cathedral style. Even in smaller communities and pockets of Polish inhabitance, there is a good chance that a Polish Cathedral will be there.

That is the case in Pulaski, Wisconsin, where there is Assumption BVM Church, a beautiful and exceptionally large church for a community of around 3,500 inhabitants. In Dubois, Illinois, seventy miles east of St. Louis, there is St. Charles Borromeo Catholic Church, patterned after St. Stanislaus in Saint Louis, and while not as big, it is still a large "cathedral" for a town of around 250 people. St. Charles can be seen from miles away.

A criticism of the ostentatious nature of the churches is that they were an over blown attempt of the poor immigrant Poles to project a higher social and cultural status than what they were. I would counter that assertion by saying these churches accurately represent the historical, ancestral, and natural self-respect and self-confidence of the Poles in a way that is no different for instance, than the immense German Gothic churches that dot the skyline in many of the large urban centers in the United States.

I never thought of the Polish Cathedrals as a singular idea, but they are another example of the legacy of the Polish immigrant experience in this country and we should cherish them and do everything we can to save every one of them.

Polish or Not?

The television sitcom *The Office* should be renamed *The Polish American Office*. Steve Carrell who plays Michael on the show is Polish on his mom's side. John Krasinski who played Jim, is Polish on his father's side. Now we find that Amy Ryan, who played Holly Flax in *The Office* and according to ethnicelebs.com was born Amy Beth Dziewiontkowski. Her grandfather was named Teofil "Theodore" Dziewiontowski.

The name Danielle Demski appeared on the Yahoo ticker recently. Her Wikipedia line is that she is a "television presenter and beauty queen from Chandler, Arizona, who has competed in the Miss Teen USA and Miss USA pageants." In fact, she is one of only seventeen contestants to have placed in both events.

Danielle is not just a pretty face though. Her attributes include a "witty personality," writing and producing, and "comfort in front of the camera." The daughter of a professional athlete and a former Arizona Cardinals cheerleader, she has found much of her employment in the sports world, but she has done commercials for Toyota, co-hosted with Nick Cannon and Wayne Grady, was a correspondent on "AXS Live," and hosted a preview of James Cameron's "Last Mysteries of the Titanic" on the Discovery Channel. One of her specialties is her inside knowledge about how Las Vegas lives and breathes.

Danielle is widely known as a Vegas expert. This led her to host the long running, syndicated "Vegas Minute," where she covered the most exclusive Sin City locations and entertainment news. In addition, she's appeared as a Vegas expert on the Travel Channel.

This is a woman who is fully engaged, check out her website (http://www.danielledemski.com), and let me know, Danielle Demski, Polish or not?

Robert Kadlec has been tapped by Health and Human Services Secretary Alex Azar to coordinate the "department's coronavirus response." He is a physician, a career officer in the United States Air Force, and was nominated by President Trump and confirmed by the U.S. Senate in 2017 to become Assistant Secretary of Health and Human Services in the Preparedness and Response division.

Kadlec said in March 2018 that his office is taking on several efforts to protect the U.S. from '21st century health security threats.' These threats could include the deployment of bioweapons (such as infectious diseases, bacteria, viruses, or toxins) or the release of chemical weapons (such as chlorine gas or mustard gas).

Kadlec is a Polish name but is Dr. Robert "I'm glad he is in charge" Kadlec, Polish, or not?

Wesolego Alleluja and God bless you this Easter. For sure, visit that Polish cathedral in your city for the sunrise Resurrection Mass. If you do, remember and please, with flu and coronavirus possibilities still around, wash your hands!!

May-June 2020

May is the month for feminism.

*I*n the Catholic tradition, May is the month for Mary, Mother of Jesus, Son of God, and having grown up in a Catholic ghetto, we always had a May crowning at our grade school in honor of her. Polish churches traditionally have a May crowning as Mary is the beloved mother, protector, and revered patron of Christian Poland. Mary was also a favorite of Saint Pope John Paul II. Pope John Paul has said that the Black Madonna Shrine, a Marian shrine, is "a bastion of faith, spirit, and culture."

For some, other Christians, even some Catholics, American progressives, and liberally minded persons in general, John Paul II, though they acknowledged him as a sincere and enthusiastic believer, was simply put, culturally and theologically backward. He was not perceived as "woke," as Pope Francis is in this country. In an article about the new book by Sue Ellen Browder, entitled, *Sex and the Catholic Feminist* (Ignatius Press/Augustine Institute, January 2020), we learn that Saint Pope John Paul II was really a feminist.

Yes, a feminist. I have not read the book and maybe this is just news to me, but what a wonderful thing, even an astounding thing, to hear about him especially in the month of May, the month for Mary. Come to think of it, I guess it is possible to make the case that Mary was a feminist in her own right. At the wedding feast in Cana (John 2:1-11), Mary tells the servants, "Do whatever he tells you." Those simple words are full of power and meaning and in a certain way, how appropriate it ties to the topic.

Browder, who is Catholic, pro-life, and calls herself a feminist, observed that "during his pontificate, John Paul II urged Catholics not to reject feminism but to embrace a 'new feminism' and, in private audiences, called himself 'the feminist pope.'" In 1988 the pope wrote the apostolic letter "Dignity and Vocation of Women", and I would encourage you to read it.

In this letter, Saint John Paul discusses many different sides of womanhood such as women as presented in scripture, women as beings juxtaposed to men, and woman, Mother of God. Here is a line from the letter, as a thought from Saint John Paul II to carry with you: "The personal resources of femininity are certainly no less than the resources of masculinity: they are merely different." Amen.

Amen I say to you, also, that Sue Ellen Browder is not the only woman that has John Paul II's back. Well before *Sex and the Catholic Feminist*, a paper appeared in *Crisis* magazine in 1997 entitled "The Pope's New Feminism" (https://www.catholiceducation.org/en/controversy/common-misconceptions/the-pope-s-new-feminism.html). It was written by Mary Ann Glendon, United States Ambassador to the Holy See from 2004 to 2009. I would encourage you to read it. This is another extraordinarily worded effort to show the Church's and especially John Paul II's attitude and concern towards women. She mentions the Pope's "new feminism" principle and adds a new dimension that speaks of his humanity and his heart.

> *By the mid-1990s, it was clear that one of the great achievements of the papacy of John Paul II has been to give greatly increased life and vigour to the Second Vatican Council's fertile statements on women. In a remarkable series of writings, he has meditated more deeply than any of his predecessors on the roles of women and men in the light of the word of God… No one who reads these messages can fail to be impressed by the evident love, empathy, and respect John Paul II holds for womankind, nowhere more manifest than in his compassionate words to unwed mothers and women who have had abortions. The image that comes through is of a man who is comfortable with women, and who listens attentively to their deepest concerns.*

The words "comfortable with women" in that last sentence is, as they say in the MasterCard commercial, priceless.

"New feminism," compassionate, comfortable, and listens are contrary to anything you would have ever heard presented in the American media, but it is refreshing to hear again how relatable Pope John Paul II was to the faithful, especially women. But we always knew that, and it ties in very nicely to a guy who professed to be "the feminist pope."

Polish or Not?

ECM stands for "Edition of Contemporary Music" and was the "inception of producer Manfred Eicher of ECM records." ECM is many things (musical classifications, recording sonics, and specific artists) but it also includes avant-garde jazz. In my *Rough Guide book of Playlists* (Rough Guides Ltd., London, 2007), the description for Jan Garbarek says, "The cathedral-toned Norwegian saxophonist… defined the 'ECM sound.'"

Garbarek, born in Mysen, Norway, in 1947 is the son of a Polish World War II prisoner of war and a "farmer's daughter" from Norway. His inspiration began as a teenager when he heard John Coltrane on the radio, and he subsequently learned to play the saxophone. His journey as a musician spans fifty-five years and over that time he has composed, conspired, and played with some of the finest musicians in the jazz world, and has incorporated a number of different influences such as Indian and Eastern music, medieval polyphony, and Scandinavian folk melodies.

He is aware of his Polish lineage as he was a regular at the Polish Jazz Jamboree in Warsaw from 1966 to 1973 and has performed several times in Poland since then. As for his ability, I did some YouTube'n to see if he is the real deal. Check him out yourself but be sure you listen to "Brother Wind March." He sounds like the real deal to me.

Remember the character Millie Swanson on *Mayberry R.F.D.*? Millie, played by Arlene Leanore Golonka, was born in Chicago in 1936 and is of Polish descent. She roomed with Valarie Harper for a time and had numerous supporting roles over the years in film and television. Besides *Mayberry*, she appeared in TV series such as *The Flying Nun*, *I Spy*, *That Girl*, *The Mary Tyler Moore Show*, *M*A*S*H*, *All in the Family*, *Taxi*, and *Murder, She Wrote*. Arlene could play cute and perky as well as sexy and had a wonderful career as an actress and as an acting coach.

Remember Mary this May, Happy Constitution Day, and hopefully by the time you receive this edition of the Polish American Journal the virus-crisis will have subsided, and we will all be enjoying the summer, out, and working, and buying stuff.

July-August 2020

Monuments and Makowiec.

Along with the COVID virus, the big news causing a lot of consternation in the United States is the removal or destruction of monuments to Confederate soldiers or politicians and of Revolutionary heroes who were slave owners or involved in the slave trade. Here is a short Polish story that might also shed light and add perspective on the debate we are having about this in our country.

When I visited Poland in the early 1980s, I was standing with an acquaintance waiting for a taxi. I spied a World War II looking monument, soldiers with guns, and fighting an enemy, across the street. I asked the person what the monument meant. Without even looking, he stared straight ahead and said, "oh, those are our heroes." Later, I found out it was about Russian soldiers "liberating" Poland from the Germans.

Most Poles consider the Russians back stabbers and invaders and so the bitter sarcasm was understandable. A portion of Americans think anyone involved with the Confederacy or slavery to be immoral. I will not opine on which monuments or statues belong, here or in Poland, and I am sympathetic to reviewing their viability. I do know that circumstances for which they were erected might not be plausible or sensible anymore.

I do know that some of the Russian memorials have been replaced with Polish heroes and famous persons and this kind of reckoning is still going on. Perhaps that is the kind of approach any country needs rather than unilaterally tearing down the structures. Tearing down, unfortunately, seems only as civilized as the ideology or action for which the old monuments were created.

The thinking part's over so let's eat!! I flipped to the Public Broadcasting Station (PBS) and there was a cooking show. I usually pause to see what they are making and this time the word Poland was mentioned by the chef. Okay, now I am really paying attention.

The chef is Alexandra August, and the show is *Flavor of Poland* (https://www.flavorofpoland.com). Two things stand out with this show about Polish cuisine. The first is that Alexandra is creating dishes in the same manner and format as some of the other television star chefs we are most familiar with. Some of my favorites are Jacques Pepin, Emeril Lagasse, Rachael Ray, and Martha Stewart. She walks you through the process by throwing in spices and ingredients, folding, kneading, and mixing. It looks very professional.

The other part of her program, at least in the one that I watched, is to impart the history of the region and method for making the dish. That matches other cooking shows I have watched especially if it is about the culinary traits of a specific region.

Pani August is a charming presenter and a thorough teacher. See the web site for videos of her episodes and some of her recipes. The presentation of the dish is very modern and inviting. Smacznego!

Polish or Not?

In just one viewing of the ethnicelebs.com website (I check this out periodically to see if any new Polish celebs have shown up), three past "Polish or not?" queries were answered. I bought a lottery ticket that same day.

In the June 2019 Pondering Pole I asked if **Chelsie Kryst**, Miss USA 2019, described as "whose dad is white and mother is African American" in Wikipedia, was Polish or not. The first clue was that "Kryst" could be a shortened version of say, "Krystkowiak" as in Larry Krystkowiak, coach of the NCAA University of Utah men's basketball team. According to ethnicelebs.com, Chelsie's father is Polish but there is no explanation for the name Kryst. Not bragging, but when my wife and I watched the pageant, I remarked throughout that Chelsie was one of my picks for the title. Beautiful, smart, exotic look, and strong personality.

Travis Kelce, tight end for the Super Bowl champs, Kansas City Chiefs, was a Polish or not request in the January 2019 Pondering Pole. Travis was born in Cleveland Heights, Ohio, a suburb of Cleveland and has a last name similar to Kielce, Poland. Ethnicelebs.com has his ethnicity as Polish, English, and Scottish but does not give the percentages of each. The focus on his Polish ethnicity is on his mother's side and some of the names listed are Sadlowsky, Olchefsky, and Petranek. Interestingly, there is no mention of where the name Kelce comes from.

She is now 17 years old, but in May of 2018 **Jo Jo Siwa**, dancer, singer, actress, and a big hair-bowed YouTube personality appeared in Polish or not. Her profile in ethnicelebs.com shows Jo Jo's father, Tom, as Polish. Her paternal grandfather is Ronald J. Siwa, the son of Andrew Siwa and Emily Bielanski, and her paternal grandmother is Joan G. Potkowski, the daughter of Joseph Potkowski and Gertrude Rakowski.

Jo Jo has won the *Nickelodeon Kids' Choice Awards* for Favorite Viral Music Artist, Favorite Musical YouTube Creator, Favorite TV Host, and Favorite Social Music Star and has a net worth of twelve million dollars. An outstanding young woman and hopefully a great future.

If you are a Seinfeld fan and you are Polish, then you know many if not all the "Polish" references. Remember the episode about the chocolate babka? Remember an early show about Jerry's immigrant relative Manya and the controversy about people who give their kids ponies? "In Poland, vee all had ponies!" cried Manya in response to Jerry's dismissive and reckless remarks. Admittedly, some other Polish characters or mentions were not cute or flattering but for those that hit a familiar and comical nerve, it was cool to hear.

It is with a sad heart that one of the main personalities of the show and I would say one of our great comedians, Jerry Stiller, who played George Costanza's father, Frank Costanza, passed away May 11th of this year. It is fitting that a show with an ample smattering of Polish references had Stiller in the cast who in fact has a Polish connection himself. From ethnicelebs.com, he is "the son of Bella (Cytrynbaum/Citrin) and William 'Willie' Stiller, a bus driver. His father was born in New York, to Jewish emigrants, from Chijika, Galicia. His mother was a Jewish emigrant, from Frampol, Poland."

Despite his on-stage persona as abrasive and crabby, "every one of his acquaintances in and out of show business swear he was the kindest and most harmless man on the planet." We are gonna miss you Jerry, but you will live on as Stiller (from *Stiller and Meara*), Frank (Frank Costanza from *Seinfeld*), and Art (Arthur Spooner from *King of Queens*).

Happy Independence Day to all, be safe (still), think and debate before tearing anything down, and if you have a thought about this month's topic, have a question, or have interesting facts to share, contact me.

September 2020

"Just another day on the job."

A doctor told me one time "stay away from doctors." I have the utmost respect and admiration for doctors, but I really do prefer to avoid them. I feel the same about cops. We respect and need them, but on balance, I do want to stay away from them if possible. In truth, they want to avoid me too.

The news these days is replete with stories about what the police are doing, what they are not doing, what they should be doing, how we should fix them, redirect them, defund them, and so on. On and on with the police and most of it is negative. It is a shame.

So, when I saw a Fox News report with Sandra Smith about the spot-on actions of a police officer in Sterling Heights, Michigan, I was pleased and warning, this story will pull heavily at your heart strings. Even Sandra advised the audience, "What you are about to see will make it hard for you to keep it together." Officer Cameron Maciejewski saved the life of a three-week-old baby.

"I was about a mile away from the house. I was right around the corner on the call when the call came out. And the only information I got from our dispatch was there's an infant not breathing, and everyone is screaming in the background," said Officer Maciejewski.

There are a host of YouTube videos showing what happened from the dashcam of the squad car showing how Maciejewski kept the mother and family calm, how he assessed the status of the child, and finally how he dislodged what was in the baby's throat. It is hard to maintain your composure when you see it.

"Very powerful," said Chief Dale Dwojakowski."I've been a police officer for 25 years. The last couple of months have been brutal, not just for me, but every cop in the United States. What a lot of people don't see is what we do every single day. Our guys do great police work including saving lives!"

Amen chief and what a credit Cameron is to your department and to all the consistent and worthy police officers protecting and serving us. Although as Officer Maciejewski said in the Smith interview, it was "just another day on the job." Sure, and thank you for your service.

For the record, on top of everything else, Sandra Smith, Chicago girl, pronounced Maciejewski's name perfectly. Thank *you* for your service, Sandy!

Polish or Not?

I am a major fan and always have a bag of baby carrots (also known as Baby Whole Carrots). There are some in the fridge to munch on as an occasional snack, but I also like them with a sandwich or soup at lunch. Come to find out, the "inventor" of the baby carrot is Michael Anthony Yurosek who passed away June 22nd, 2005. He was the son of Polish immigrants from Javoshinka, Poland, and according to his obit, he and "his twin brother began school not speaking a word of English."

Mike excelled in athletics and started and ran businesses with his older brother John (Yurosek Brothers Farms in Newhall, California) and in 1969 formed a company called Yurosek and Son, Inc., with his son David. In 1974, this corporation later moved to Lamont, California, and it "became one of the largest carrot operations in the nation." This is where the Baby Whole Carrots were "discovered." Yurosek in Lamont was sold to Grimmway Farms of Arvin, California in 1995.

Quite a guy and life well lived and you can read his obit at https://www.legacy.com/obituaries/bakersfield/obituary.aspx?n=michael-anthony-yurosek&pid=14328085.

Another Yurosek is famous but has nothing to do with carrots. I am watching the Turner Classic Movie channel and it is Gary Lockwood night. Lockwood, an actor in film and television from 1958 to 1998, was born John Gary Yurosek in 1937. Besides acting, his other claim to fame is that he is the nephew of Michael Yurosek of Whole Baby Carrots fame, just mentioned.

Gary was a sharp looking dude in the day and had a credible body of work appearing in movies such as *2001: A Space Odyssey*, *Star Trek* "Where No Man Has Gone Before," and *The Lieutenant*. Oh, and just one more claim to fame, at least to me, is that he was married to Stephanie Powers from 1966 to 1972. Gary Lockwood, Polish and husband of Stephanie Powers, also Polish.

The name Leonard Soloway popped up on an Amazon Prime list of documentary films. The movie is called *Leonard Soloway's Broadway*. I am a musicals guy (season ticket holder to The MUNY – St. Louis Municipal Opera Theatre for over 20 years) and was curious to watch the movie and was more curious about the man. The Leonard Soloway story is about the "legendary" impact he has had on the greatest theatre district in the United States, Broadway, in Midtown Manhattan, New York City.

Here is a quick summary of his achievements from his website (https://www.leonardsolowaysbroadway.com/bio):

Leonard Soloway is a Broadway Producer whose career spans 70 years and over 100 productions. A native of Cleveland his personal life story and professional accomplishments take one on a journey from the very beginning of the Off-Broadway scene to the world of smash hits that made Broadway history. His work has been honored with Tony Awards and Pulitzer Prizes and he has worked with many of the brightest creative talents on the Great White Way including Jerome Robbins, Colleen Dewhurst, Jason Robards and Paul Newman.

In the movie it says that Leonard's father emigrated from Russia but in an email from Jeffrey Lesser, his nephew, Mr. Soloway maintains the family was from Poland. He is the son of Mayer Judd Solowejagh who was born in the Russian occupied part of Poland in 1903. After World War I the family left Poland and moved to South America. They later emigrated to the United States and the rest is history for Leonard.

From *Leonard Soloway's Broadway*, he is called a "gentleman," "at 90, a familiar face on the Broadway scene," and "a Broadway legend." An honorable and successful man, a legend, and we thank him for all that he has contributed to American culture. See the movie. Better yet, see a Soloway musical on Broadway.

Here is a surprise. Professional hockey star Mike Bossy claims a Polish connection. He is Polish/Ukrainian on his father's side according to Ethnicelebs.com. His paternal grandfather "was named Walter Vladimir Bossy. Walter was from Jaslo, Podkarpackie, Poland." Among a plethora of awards, honors,

THE PONDERING POLE 2   2020–2023 and "BEST OF"

and trophies, Mike has been named one of the "100 Greatest NHL Players" of all time.

Ah, those one-name music stars. Cher, Madonna, Prince, Kiesza, and now Szlachetka (shla-het'-ka). You have a lot of confidence to only be known by the name Szlachetka, for several reasons, but all I can say is "you go!!" He has carved out his musical career in country western and has received a number of accolades, the best coming from Rolling Stone magazine who proclaimed him one of "The Top New Country Artists You Need To Know."

Matthew Szlachetka was born in Massachusetts where he started his career and then moved to Los Angeles honing his skills. He now calls home Nashville, Tennessee, *the* place for Country. In his third album, *Young Heart, Old Soul,* the songs draw from his life journey as it "unfolds like the soundtrack to a cross-country road trip. Filled with heartland hooks, folk melodies, and searing electric guitar, these songs draw a line between Los Angeles – where Szlachetka lived for years, soaking up the warm harmonies and jangling riffs of the city's folk-rock icons – and his new home in Nashville, TN, the epicenter of modern-day Americana."

November 2020

A 1496 Project?

From Wikipedia: According to historian Edward Corwin the year 1496 (Statutes of Piotrków) marks the proper beginning of the serfdom era in Poland.

You might be familiar with The 1619 Project which is a movement to designate the birth of the United States from the time that the first slaves landed on American soil rather than the year 1776, the date marking the split of the colonies from English rule. For those espousing The 1619 Project, the importance of slavery supersedes the American independence from England in 1776.

Slavery was the cruelest form of human control as the person was owned by the master and the slave had no rights. Serfdom as practiced throughout Europe including in Poland (panszczyzna) was second to it. In Poland, throughout the Piast Dynasty up until the end of the 15th century, peasant classes were mobile, allowed to own land, and had certain, though limited, legal rights against feudal lords. Not an easy life of course, but one with some freedom from those in power above.

With the rise of the Polish-Lithuanian Commonwealth, serfdom heightened and proliferated resulting in harsh punishments for indiscretions, little legal recrimination against the landowner (szlachta), tighter regulations or no possibility on movement and education, and mandates on where serfs could obtain alcohol or other goods (propination).

A good read on the specifics of serfdom in Poland is in an article by Mikolaj Glinski at https://culture.pl/en/article/slavery-vs-serfdom-or-was-poland-a-colonial-empire. Serfdom ran the gamut from grim to cruel as a condition imposed on the Polish peasantry and what the ramifications on the populace at large are fodder for sociologist and psychologists.

THE PONDERING POLE 2   2020–2023 and "BEST OF"

Ironically, the law ending serfdom in Poland (1864) closely followed the Emancipation Proclamation (1862) in the United States although vestiges of it continued into the 1900s just as Jim Crow and discrimination followed blacks into the 1960s.

I remember the vestiges from my past. This goes back many years ago. I was listening to one of our older parishioners disconcerted and in a tizzy. To illustrate his point, he shouted how "the szlachta would beat us while riding on their horses!" Something to that affect and for what seemed like a minor offense. I do not know if any of my ancestors were serfs, but I am inclined to believe they were.

Do we need a 1496 Project? For myself, I am still working on how much of an impact this has had on my whole being with counseling and Belvedere martinis. Beyond that, I believe my family and my extended Polonian community has recovered well (in some cases very well) making the best of whatever freedoms were available and taking advantage of opportunities and optimism wherever they could find them both here and in Poland.

Whatever you think, serfdom is a fascinating subject and certainly worth – pondering.

Polish or Not?

Are you like me and don't start thinking about Christmas (especially the gifts) until after Thanksgiving? While I do like the designated calendar barrier between these two giant holidays, the time rush till Christmas is getting smaller and harder. Tell yourself, tell me, to get a jump on it this year and if you have small ones to buy for, how about some children's books? May I suggest any of the forty New York Times best-selling Jarrett Krosoczka "books for young readers, including his wildly popular Lunch Lady graphic novels," *Hey, Kiddo*, and others.

Jarrett had anything but a simple life growing up (an "unconventional childhood") and was raised by his maternal grandparents, Joe and Shirley Krosoczka. His mom struggled with addiction, and it was drawing and creating stories from the pictures that helped him cope.

He is a graduate of the Rhode Island School of Design, is a teacher at Montserrat College of Art, and "was chosen by Print as one of their 20 Top New Visual Artists Under 30." There is a TED talk by him on YouTube which I recommend you see as he explains his life and what made him go on. Quite a life that now is lemonade and you can learn more about it at http://www.studiojjk.com. Polish name but is Jarrett Krosoczka, Polish or not?

There was a part of me that was hoping for a culturally Polish, Polish connected, or at the least, an Eastern European person to fill the Supreme Court vacancy left by the passing of Justice Ruth Bader Ginsberg who I really did not know much about. We are sorry for the loss, and I am sure her replacement, Amy Barrett, if confirmed, will be a solid jurist. As it turns out however, Justice Ginsberg has a link to Poland anyway. From ethnicelebs.com,

Her father, Nathan Bader, was a Russian Jewish emigrant, born in Podolsk. Her mother, Celia (Amster), was born in New York, to Polish Jewish parents... Justin Ginsburg's patrilineal line can be traced to Salomon Bader, who was born, c. 1759, in Kraków, Kraków County, Lesser Poland Voivodeship, Poland, and to his father Samuel Bader. Justice Ginsburg's paternal grandfather was Samuel "Sam" Bader (the son of Isaac/Isaak Moses/Moyzesz Bader and Yetta Levy). Isaac was born in Warsaw, Poland, the son of Mendel Samuel Bader and Yocheved/Jachwet Birnbaum.

December 2020

Warsaw Cool.

Most of us know where the Polish neighborhoods are (or were) in the big cities of the United States. Greenpoint in Brooklyn, Polish Hill in Pittsburgh, Pole Town in Detroit, Logan Square in Chicago, and the Nordeast in Minneapolis. This is just a small sample and some of them I was fortunate to have visited and relish over the years.

I love the neighborhood idea and scene. This is not to be confused with the strictly tourist places which are wonderful and worth seeing but neighborhoods are where the people live and are the true pulse of the community. We are blessed in Saint Louis to have several urban style "areas" and neighborhoods. Areas that have names such as The Central West End, Grand Center, Downtown, the Southside, and the Northside. Within each are one or several neighborhoods with names like Dutch Town, Italian Hill, The Ville, Soulard, and The Grove. Some are quaint, some ethnic, some visually appealing, and some for a great mix of bars, restaurants, and nightlife. All are composed of a set of people, a special vibe, and there are those that are simply relaxed and familiar places to live.

I started thinking, what are the best neighborhoods in Poland? Are there any and are they equivalent to our cool and fun neighborhoods in the U.S.? My online searching converged at two places. The first is from the Nomadlist travel website (https://nomadlist.com/neighborhoods/warsaw) which has information "for almost every major town and city in the world with a significant population." The other is a March 2017 article by Marta Podeszwa entitled The Coolest Neighborhoods in Warsaw (https://theculturetrip.com/europe/poland/articles/the-10-coolest-neighbourhoods-in-warsaw) which lists and briefly describes ten great neighborhoods within Warsaw's metropolitan limits.

Warsaw is divided into eighteen districts or areas similar to Saint Louis. The Nomadlist neighborhood page is a map of the city's districts and for instance, the main or primary district is called Srodmiescie (downtown). It was a delight for me as one who once visited the capital city as a tourist to see the map and find and relive some of the sites but also because it allowed for matching to the Podeszwa picks in her coolest article to see where they are located and give the venue perspective. This is an excellent platform for exploring Warsaw online and I would recommend you try this website not only for Warsaw but for other Polish cities before traveling.

One neat feature of Nomadlist is the "tags" button that activates and deactivates overlays of certain areas with descriptive text and highlights. For instance, parts of the city are tagged "hipster district," "dogs everywhere," "gentrification role model," "upcoming area," and "the most underrated place." It is an interesting and potentially useful feature.

Here are some of the "coolest" neighborhoods in Warsaw according to Marta Podeszwa to keep in mind for your next visit.

Plac Zbawiciela (Savior Square) is in the southwest part of the Srodmiescie or downtown district and is not that far from the famous Chopin statue. Zbawiciela is "a magnet to Warsaw's hipsters" and the Church of the Holiest Savior borders one side of the square. It is also "home to the trendy wine bar and café Charlotte."

Plac Grzybowski in the western part of the downtown district is "part of the Old Jewish Quarter, centered around the grand Renaissance All Saints Church," and "has recently experienced a lot of redevelopment and become one of the coolest areas." There are "great dining options on the nearby Prozna Street which is made up of beautifully restored tenement houses."

Poznanska Street is part of another neighborhood you might want to hang out. According to Podeszwa, it "is one of the liveliest streets of the central Srodmiescie district, popular both among the locals and visitors." It has various ethnic restaurants, art galleries, and includes the "fine dining restaurant Nolita (on the nearby Wilcza Street)… "

The Praga district which is across the Vistula River from Srodmiescie has two cool neighborhoods: Zabkowska Street "where you will find a raft of alternative bars and cafés… ," and the Soho Factory complex which is "a mix of post-industrial buildings and new developments… " It is also the place for "one of the city's best Polish restaurants, Warszawa Wschodnia."

Zoliborz is a district and a neighborhood north of downtown. Per Podeszwa, it "is one of Warsaw residents' favorite places to live and hang out. It boasts a village feel thanks to its quiet charming streets (make sure you walk around the area's most beautiful streets such as Brodzinskiego and Wieniawskiego)… " I can think of four or five older neighborhoods in Saint Louis that match that type and description.

Other places Marta and others I surveyed have cited are Mokotow, Saska Kepa, Francuska Street, Wisla Left Bank, and Konstancin. I hope you read the Podeszwa article and check out some of these places on your next visit to Poland and Warsaw. If you do, let me know what you think. Let me also know if you have a favorite "cool" neighborhood of your own in Warsaw or anywhere else in Poland.

At the least, there is a neighborhood you can visit in your mind and heart for sure and that is Bethlehem. Wesolych Swiat to all the *Pondering Pole* readers and my wish is that you have a wonderful and blessed Christmas despite any current difficulties or hardships you have endured or are enduring.

III
2021

January 2021

1. d4 d5 2. c4

These three moves constitute what is known in chess as the Queen's Gambit.

Like many other things in life, there was a time when I got somewhat interested in chess. Not seriously interested because I was not 1. Super consumed with it like I was with baseball and football, and 2. I did not take the time to *learn* about it. If you want to be good at something, learn about it, understand it, and then practice. Checkmate on the Pondering Pole for chess.

There is a mini-series on Netflix called *The Queen's Gambit* and more on that later. My interest in Polish chess Grandmasters came independent of the series but I was pleasantly surprised by both. You can find a list of all chess Grandmasters by nation in Wikipedia and the Russians are number one in this category. You will recognize some of the greatest names of course: Gary Kasparov, Anatoly Karpov, and then there is Boris Spassky who was a world champion and battled American Bobby Fischer in some epic matches. But the Poles have held their own over the years. I counted about fifty since they started recognizing this achievement.

Of the current top twenty players in the world (www.jagranjosh.com/general-knowledge/list-of-top-20-chess-players-in-the-world-1595223383-1), at number 16, is a Pole, Jan-Krzysztof Duda. Another notable Grandmaster from the past and one that ties in well with *The Queen's Gambit* series is a Polish woman, Monika Socko. Ms. Socko (nee' Bobrowska) is married to Grandmaster Bartosz Socko and was born March 24, 1978. She has garnered the title Polish women's chess champion eight times. Her last victory was in 2017.

She also "won the gold medal at the Women's European Team Chess Championship in 2005," and a couple silvers in the same tournament years later, and in 2013, she scored a bronze medal. In 2002 she won the bronze in the Women's Chess Olympiad. Among her peers, Monika Socko has excelled in chess, is worthy of the title Grandmaster, and is an example to all young women and especially young Polish woman.

If you like binge TV then you might want to try *The Queen's Gambit*, now showing on Netflix. If you have seen the series *Mad Men*, then *Queen's Gambit* is very much like that only it is about mad women. Lots of drinking, drugs, incessant smoking, but instead of the show revolving around an ad agency, this one is about pawns and bishops. The other thing both shows have in common is the main character of *Gambit*, Beth Harmon (played by Anya Taylor-Joy) favors (in my opinion) the looks of the character Joan Holloway, played by Christina Hendricks. The face mainly. Judge for yourself.

For our purposes though, the revelation for me is the Polish born actor, Marcin Dorocinski, who plays the Russian Grandmaster Vasily Borgov. While he does not have a lot of lines and does not get that much screen time, his steely-eyed focus and good looks make him stand out. You can find out more about Dorocinski in Wikipedia and there is short feature article online about him from The First News published out of Poland (www.thefirstnews.com/article/marcin-dorocinski-woos-fans-in-netflix-hit-the-queens-gambit-but-who-is-he-17303).

The 47-year-old was born in Milanowek, near Warsaw, is a dog lover, and aspired to playing pro soccer until he blew out his knee. Needing a real job, Marcin enrolled in the Aleksander Zelwerowicz State Theatre Academy. That was in 1993 and 27 years later Dorocinski is still working in television, film, and theatre. While acting hasn't provided a blockbuster hit, it has sustained him and his family and he has a net worth of $2 million (Celebritynetworth.com). His television and film resume are listed in Wikipedia and I have already made a note to see him in the movie *Spies of Warsaw*.

I hope *The Queen's Gambit* leads to more and better work for this talented and handsome guy. Good luck Marcin!!

February 2021

Father Dzierozynski: a worthy life.

Missed mentioning this last month. How about a few Polish New Year resolutions.

1) I do not hear it much anymore but try steering away from "I'm proud to be Polish." No other ethnic group says "I'm proud" unless they have a deep-seated inferiority complex. They are just Black, Asian, Italian, Jewish, or Irish. Pride is one of the deadly sins anyway. Simply stated, you are what you are and that is it. What you become is all you with Polish factored in.

2) Learn how to pronounce the names properly. Anglicizing is accepted of course but knowing the real pronunciation should be a part of who you are. A part of who YOU are. Takes a little work but Polish can be relatively easy to learn and pronounce and useful where Polish "is spoken."

3) Resolve, and this applies to anything in your life, if you want or need something done, do it yourself. If you think Stan or Jadzia or Brian or Ashley is going to do it, they might, but more than likely they won't. Get involved. Take it on.

4) Knowing the history and culture are so important for your emotional, psychological, and intellectual well-being. To illustrate, here is an excerpt from a recent political presentation:

> *... If you have no idea what came before you, you have no idea of what normal is and you cannot understand the consequences of what is happening now. If you can't look to the past [then you can't] understand the consequences of the same behavior in another time. The root of wisdom is knowing what happened before, I mean, that is the road map.*

Our history and culture seem to be well documented so there are abundant choices. It truly will help you understand the "road map."

For instance, in his book, *Poland, A History* (a must read), the author Adam Zamoyski says this: "In 1564 Hosius brought the Jesuits to Poland, to re-conquer the hearts, and more specifically the minds, of the Poles… " Thus, Cardinal Stanislaw Hosius, seemingly a great man for various reasons, established the Society of Jesus in Poland where they would be important and significant initially for the Counter-Reformation and for centuries there-after. This sets the stage and narrative for the life of Franciszek Dzierozynski, "a Polish Catholic priest and Jesuit who became a prominent missionary to the United States."

I learned about Father Dzierozynski many years ago as being connected to the founding of St. Louis University. Lately I saw his name in a book by local radio talk show host Charlie Brennan called *Amazing St. Louis* (Reedy Press, Saint Louis, 2013). The chapter involving Dzierozynski is entitled "Jesuits Built SLU (St. Louis University) with slaves." That does not sound good for 1) the Catholic order Society of Jesus owning slaves, and 2) for Father Dzierozynski to be involved with it. Hold on, there is more good from this story than the title lends.

Brennan got his material for this chapter from a historian by the name of C. Walker Gollar. Most of the bad stuff that happened to the slaves (before working on the site that eventually would become SLU in 1829) was when the Jesuits initially settled in Florissant, Missouri (located ten miles from St. Louis) in 1823 and it derived from the priest in charge, Father Charles Van Quickenborne. He was tough and unyielding in his temperament and even cruel in his treatment of the slaves. Slaves were used to serve at the "priests' farm" in Florissant known as St. Stanislaus Jesuit Novitiate which later became St. Stanislaus Seminary. The building is currently used by the Missouri Department of Conservation. However, concerning Father Dzierozynski,

> **In 1847, the superior of the United States Society of Jesus, Francis Dzierozynski, visited Florissant and ordered improvements to the slave' inadequate quarters. He also granted approval for one slave to return to Maryland to visit his children – a directive Father Van Quickenborne ignored.**

Father Dzierozynski also "instructed the St. Louis Jesuits to only sell their slaves with his permission and then only 'to humane and Christian masters' who would purchase them for their own use." We can analyze why these religious people would own slaves, what was their rationale, and whether this simply was just another strange chapter in the life of the church. On balance though, the life, career, and accomplishments of Francis Dzierozynski are admirable. Maybe even worthy.

Father Dzierosynski was born January 3, 1779, in Orsha, at that time part of the Russian Empire. In 1806 he joined the Society of Jesus religious order and furthered his studies and taught in Polotsk and Mogliev in Russia and in Bologna, Italy. In 1820 he was sent as a missionary to America and in 1823 "he was appointed the superior of the Maryland Mission, with jurisdiction over all the Jesuits in the United States."

During his term as the superior of the order, he continued teaching at Georgetown College in Georgetown, Kentucky, "reconciled the Society of Jesus and the Corporation of Roman Catholic Clergymen," and as previously mentioned, was involved in the management of the Florissant and St. Louis facilities in Missouri. His administration in the affairs of the Jesuits in the United States had him directly involved with people such as John Quincy Adams, Roger Taney, Henry Clay, and Pope Pius VII.

During and outside his time as superior of the order, I realize that this man was a fighter for things he thought was right, progressive in his thinking on some issues, and he was at the core and in the spirit of the Jesuits, a teacher and spiritual leader of men and women. To summarize his life in a few words, he took his vocation to heart, and he made a difference.

Polish or Not?

The *Goodbye Girl* is Polish! Or is she? Marsha Mason, born April 3, 1942, (in St. Louis, Missouri no less!!), is an American actress, director, and businesswoman. I fell in love with her when I saw her in the movie *The Goodbye Girl* with Richard Dreyfuss in 1977. Other well-known films she appeared in are *Cinderella Liberty*, *Only When I Laugh*, and *Blume in Love*. She was nominated four times for the Academy Awards, won two Golden Globes, and received an Emmy for her work in the television show *Frazier*, playing the character Sherry Dempsey. Sherry was the girlfriend of Martin Crane, Frazier Crane's father, a character I found fun and appealing.

Marsha has had quite a career in film, theatre, and television and we salute her for it. Her mother is Jacqueline Helena Rakowski. Marsha Mason, Polish or not?

The October Polish or Not? featured partners or spouses of famous people who were Polish. Here is another one with a twist. James Gandolfini is actor of high repute mostly for his role in the television series *The Sopranos*. He was married to Marcy Wudarski and they had a son together, Michael Gandolfini.

According to ethnicelebs.com, Marcy is mostly Polish and a quarter Slovak (Wudarski, Chyczewski, Orosky, Pavlisko) which makes Michael about half Polish. He is an up-and-coming new face in Hollywood with a famous father. Good luck Michael.

Happy Valentine's Day and if you are a target, I hope Cupid's arrow finds you. Whatever your status, give someone a bouquet or a box of chocolates. Start 2021 off with a small act of love and kindness.

March 2021

A rule to live by.

A shared cultural system stabilizes human interaction but is also a system of value – a hierarchy of value, where some things are given priority and importance and others are not… In the West, we have been withdrawing from our tradition-, religion-, and even nation-centered cultures partly to decrease the danger of group conflict. But we are increasingly falling prey to the desperation of meaninglessness, and that is no improvement at all.

Jordan Peterson, 12 Rules for Life

The quote above is from the introduction by Jordan Peterson in his book, *12 Rules for Life, An Antidote to Chaos* (Random House Canada, 2018), and is directly applicable to those of us with "nation-centered cultures." If you are looking for a reason to hold on to at least some aspects or "traditions" of your ethnic background, or even your American background, this is confirmation to do so from someone who has studied shared cultural systems very much. *12 Rules* topped best-seller lists in three countries including the United States and sold over 3 million copies so we can assume he has at least some semblance of what he is talking about. Keeping at least one toe in the ancestral waters is a good thing in my opinion.

Peterson says the reason for "withdrawing" from shared cultural systems is to avoid group conflict. We shy away from identifying from a group so as not to seem like we are rejecting or dismissing others who are not in our group. On the other hand, "identity politics" is used to shame or accuse or get an advantage over those not in the group deemed to be unworthy or deficient. This is so real for our current American social experience. We are living it. The concept of group identity is something that Peterson addresses and references as "minimal group identification," a concept attributed to a social psychologist Henri Tajfel.

THE PONDERING POLE 2   2020–2023 and "BEST OF"

Henri Tajfel (real name Hersz Mordche) was born in Poland June 22, 1919, in Wloclawek, Poland. Tajfel grew up in Poland but left due to the Jewish *numerus clausus* restrictions to study in France at the Sorbonne University. At the outbreak of World War II, he joined the French army and was captured but survived the war in multiple concentration camps. He lost all his immediate family and many friends to the Holocaust and would "write later about the profound effect that this had on him and how it led to his later work on the psychology of prejudice and intergroup relations."

From *12 Rules*, Peterson explains "minimal group identification" by saying,

> *Tajfel's studies demonstrated two things: first, that people are social; second, that people are antisocial. People are social because they like the members of their own group. People are antisocial because they don't like the members of other groups.*

According to Jordan Peterson and by extension Henri Tajfel, identifying with group and therefore the characteristics that personify it such as traditions, religion, or nation-centered culture are good so long as they logically follow with acknowledgement and tolerance for the others. The aspects of shared cultural systems are all around us. Various races and ethnicities enjoy rooting for the Red Sox; different sexes work for the success of The Home Depot, Inc.; and waves of Polish immigrants rally around the same Polish or American flag even though their histories and experiences are dissimilar.

Group identification has great benefit and potential if understood and utilized properly. Most of us certainly know it can make life meaningful and rich and it is important that we hold on to it. So, hold on to it.

Polish or Not?

I am an enthusiastic supporter of the Crazy Horse Memorial, sculpted by Korczak Ziolkowski, and located in the Black Hills of South Dakota. This family and cultural project is as big as the mountain depicting the "Oglala Lakota warrior, Crazy Horse, riding a horse and pointing to his tribal land," One day I will see it in person.

There is another Ziolkowski that has made a major mark in an important and special way not as a sculptor but as a writer. Dr. Alekandra Ziolkowska-Boehm is the niece of Korczak Ziolkowski, has written over 30 books in both Polish and English, and has received numerous awards including most recently the Gold Cross of Merit, Turzanski Foundation Literary Award, Witness to History/Swiadek Historii Award, and in 2020, Outstanding Pole Abroad Award.

You can read more about her life and achievements in Wikipedia, and she is also featured in the Winter 2020 issue of Polish Heritage published by the American Council for Polish Culture. Start reading her books while we wait to hear about the next "monumental" Ziolkowski to emerge.

The spouses and partners of American celebrities keep coming. Jane Hajduk is an American actress and the wife of Tim Allen, the star of television sitcoms *Home Improvement* and *Last Man Standing* and of numerous popular movies including *For Richer or Poorer* and *Crazy on the Outside*. Jane has 17 credits in television and film herself including the movie *Zoom* in 2006 and Ultimate Spider-Man in 2005.

According to ethnicelebs.com, Jane was born in Oil City, Pennsylvania, October 26, 1966 and is 75% Polish. "Her paternal grandparents were born in Poland and were listed as Polish speakers on the 1930 U.S. Census." Her maternal grandmother Helen is the daughter of Felix Feroz and Eleanore Gabryszewski, both born in Poland.

Since climate change initiatives are such a big part of the new Biden administration, I checked Wikipedia to see if there is a famous Polish climate scientist or even any at all. Under the search "List of Climate Scientists," there are none that are tied to the country of Poland (Nigeria, Wales, and Armenia are represented) and only one I noticed had a Polish name. That one belongs to Micha Tomkiewicz. He has an interesting and perhaps unbelievable story.

Marcelli Robert "Micha" Tomkiewicz was born May 25, 1939 in Warsaw, Poland. At one point during the early part of World War II, he and his family were moved to the Warsaw Ghetto and then were transferred to the Bergen-Belsen concentration camp. The family was rescued by the American 743rd Tank Battalion on a train headed for the Theresienstadt camp at the end of the war. Having survived, "they soon relocated to Palestine to rebuild their lives."

Tomkiewicz is a professor and researcher and has promoted the issue of global warming. He is an authority on climate change and authored the book, *Climate Change: The Fork at the End of Now* (Momentum Press, 2011). If you know of any other renowned Polish climatologist or Global Warming expert, let me know. We, and Poland, need more of them on the list.

April 2021

The four P's.

Within a week, this is what I heard or came across about prayer, palate, purpose, and perseverance. Add or change your own P as needed.

On Sunday, a lady from church was talking about the prayer of Sister Faustina Kowalska often said at the bed of a dying person and how its calming effect and spiritual "release" were powerful. I believe she was talking about the Divine Mercy Chaplet. This was at a non-Polish church.

The February 2021 edition of *Feast* magazine (feastmagazine.com), published and distributed for foodies living in Missouri, Eastern Kansas, and Southern Illinois mentioned the Café Poland, located in Columbia, Missouri (also previously highlighted in *The Pondering Pole*). "Café Poland is perhaps best known for its pierogis, but it's lecho will make any cold winter night more enjoyable." Lecho (leczo) is a stew made of spicy bell peppers, kielbasa, and potatoes. Sounds like an alternative or a compliment to bigos and there are recipes on the web.

Bob Stockdale, a popular financial guru in St. Louis was remarking on the astute saving and investing sense of Rob Gronkowski, tight end, and Super Bowl champion for the Tampa Bay Buccaneers who has an estimated net worth of between 45 and 60 million dollars. The story is that Rob banked his salary throughout his professional football career while living solely off endorsements and other income streams. I know he has not wasted his talents on the field, but I also hope he will not bury his other "talents" in the sand rather than making meaningful and productive use of those as well. That said, there is a philosophical lesson for young Polish kids and for all kids about work and how to save and invest those precious checks.

Finally, we hear now that Theodor Geisel, aka Dr. Suess, is accused of being a racist and some or all his books are going to be removed from eBay and Amazon. Perhaps one of, if not the greatest children's book authors has fallen prey to cancel culture. However, while they are at it, can eBay and

Amazon remove the negative and stereotypical Polak joke books in their catalogue? The Larry Wilde "Official" joke books? Granted, some of Geisel's past references and characterizations are not acceptable or preferred for the current era, but his beliefs and intentions were not racist. The Wilde "dumb" Polish stuff though, is bigoted. More on Dr. Suess later.

Otherworldly Poles.

News of the Mars rover Perseverance mission "un-earthed" names of Poles in America and Poland who are or were involved since the dawn of the modern space exploration period. All can be found in Wikipedia and astronauts can be found under a "List of Astronauts by Name" search result. Here are some of those individuals.

Steve Jurczyk became the acting director of NASA (National Aeronautics and Space Administration) January 20, 2021 and this was just in time to oversee the Mars rover Perseverance mission. It was a successful operation and landing on February 18, 2021. He is 55 years old and has climbed the ladder of aeronautic research and development on the way to this current position. From an article in the Am-Pol Eagle (https://ampoleagle.com/biden-congratulates-polam-over-nasaHs-successful-mars-landing-p15159-129.htm) by Robert Strybel,

> *Jurczyk began his NASA career in 1988 at Langley Research Center in the Electronic Systems Branch as a design, integration and testing engineer developing several space-based Earth remote sensing systems. From 2002 to 2004, Jurczyk was director of engineering, and from 2004 to 2006 he was director of research and technology at Langley where he led the organizations' contributions to a broad range of research, technology and engineering disciplines contributing to all NASA mission areas.*
>
> *From August 2006, Jurczyk served as Langley's Deputy Center Director. In May 2014, Jurczyk was appointed as Director at NASA's Langley Research Center. There, he headed NASA's first field Center, which plays a critical role in NASA's aeronautics research, exploration, and science missions.*

THE PONDERING POLE 2 2020–2023 and "BEST OF"

Steve has received several awards and citations, was inspired by the pictures of Neil Armstrong and Buzz Aldrin walking on the moon, and is keenly aware of his Polish ancestry. "In 2019, Jurczyk visited the homeland of his Polish immigrant ancestors to attend the European Rover Challenge in the south-central city of Kielce." We wish Steve good luck in the new job and hope he gets appointed permanently to the directorship.

Probably the biggest name on either side of the Atlantic in Polish spaceflight history is Miroslaw Hermaszewski as the "only Polish national in space when he flew aboard the Soviet Soyuz 30 spacecraft in 1978. He was the 89th human to reach outer space."

A survivor of the Volhynian massacres by Ukrainian nationalists during World War II, he later became interested in aviation and completed a commission as a pilot in the Polish Air Force, flying over thirteen different kinds of gliders and aircraft including the F-16 and F-18 jets. "In 1976, he was chosen from a pool of 500 Polish military pilots to take part in the Interkosmos space programme," sponsored and promoted by the Soviet Union to involve associate Warsaw Pact and other allied countries in Soviet space missions. He is one of the greats.

Hermaszewski's backup for the Soyuz 30 mission was Polish astronaut Zenon Jankowski.

There are several Polish American astronauts on the list such as Karol Bobko (previously featured in the Polish American Journal), Scott Parazynski, M.D., James Pawelczyk, and George Zamka. You can review their histories and accomplishments in Wikipedia or other sources however, of these, Scott Parazynski, M.D. is probably the most impressive.

Most impressive. First, let me say, Scott needs to get a life or perhaps life has gotten too much of him. He was educated literally all over the world, is a mountain climber (Everest), a teacher, a pilot, a scuba diver, a medical doctor, and an astronaut. Oh, he is also an Eagle Scout. He is "a veteran of five Space Shuttle flights and seven spacewalks… In May 2016 he was inducted into the United States Astronaut Hall of Fame."

He traces his Polish ancestry back to his great-great-grandparents who immigrated from Krakow. The same place where Copernicus hung out.

2021

Polish or Not?

If you are in need to watch another fascinating documentary about American life, then I recommend you see *Hitsville: The Making of Motown* on Amazon Prime. The film centers on Berry Gordy and the many people that helped him succeed at giving us beautiful soulful music.

Barney Ales was one of those hired in the early years to act as a liaison between Gordy's niche (at the time) enterprise and the "wider, white-dominated music industry in the U.S." Barney was born Baldassare "Barney" Ales in Detroit. His father was Sicilian-born Silvestro Ales and his mother was "Evelyn from Northern Michigan." Much was said about the ethnicity on his father's side. Nothing about mother that I can find and from pictures it looks like Ales has blond hair. Curious to know if mom, Evelyn, is Polish or not? Poppa was a rolling stone; what was momma?

Jon Scieszka, along with Theodor Geisel/Dr. Suess can be found on the list of *The 100 Best Children's Books of All Time* (https://time.com/100-best-childrens-books). Jon was born September 8, 1954 in Flint, Michigan, and is the grandson (on his father's side) of Michael and Anna who "came to America from Poland. 'Scieszka' is a word in Polish. It means 'path.'"

Scieszka's *The True Story of the Three Little Pigs* comes in at #8 on the list, you can find out more about him on his website (http://www.jsworldwide.com/just_the_facts.html), or check out his story and many of the kid's books he has written or edited on Wikipedia.

Coming in at #1 on the list for his work, *Where the Wild Things Are*, is Maurice Sendak, born Maurice Bernard Sendak, June 10, 1928. "Sendak was born in Brooklyn, New York, to Polish-Jewish immigrant parents…"

May-June 2021

"One of the great poems of the world."

So, I am driving around in the neighborhood one day and I spot a painting, a print, of what I thought was Rembrandt van Rijn's *A Polish Nobleman*. I was convinced of it. Someone was throwing it out with the trash, so I grabbed it. I cleaned it up and used it as the centerpiece for the Poniewaz Family Golf & Reunion group picture that year. We gathered around it, cracks were flying why Cousin Eddie brought a picture of our long lost dead relative Uncle Zbigniew, and the bar maid snapped the picture.

Later I found out it was actually Rembrandt's *The Man with the Golden Helmet*. Close enough. I still have the *Golden Helmet* hanging on the wall with other pictures and paintings.

For Constitution month, if you want to meditate on *A Polish Nobleman*, go for it. That is an interesting and significant work. Might I also suggest though that you watch the YouTube presentation of *Cocktails with a Curator*, sponsored by The Frick Collection, about the painting called *The Polish Rider* (https://youtu.be/NotIFQRPnjo). *The Polish Rider* has been designated by art historian Kenneth Clark as "One of the great poems of the world."

The episode is hosted by Xavier F. Salomon, the Peter Jay Sharp Chief Curator of the museum, and he speaks about the history and impact of many of the paintings and pieces in the collection. He does this only after describing the ingredients for making an appropriate cocktail for the subject. In the case of *The Polish Rider* the drink he chose is szarlotka, made with 1/3 Zubrowka (Bison Grass) vodka, and 2/3 chilled freshly pressed apple juice/cider, with a pinch of ground cinnamon.

The Polish Rider is a famous painting with the subject being a young man, atop a horse, dressed in the Polish military style with head dress, coat (zupan), and armed with weapons of seventeenth century Poland, two carabellas (swords), and a nadziak (horseman's pick). The scene is dark, having a foreboding quality, and he is gazing back or to his side, looking for something.

It is the "looking for something" that focusses our attention and makes art historians stay up at night, maybe for centuries. The historical perspective, not mentioned in *Cocktails*, should be acknowledged. One thing you could do is read chapter nine, *A Biblical Flood*, of Adam Zamoyski's *Poland, A History* (Hippocrene Books, New York, 2012). That would give you the whole story of 17th century Poland but in summary, the young lisowczyk (light cavalry) soldier is probably looking for the enemy that could be in the form of a Cossack, a Swede, a Russian, an Ottoman Turk, or a Tartar. 17th century Poland, as Rembrandt undoubtedly knew, was a turbulent and dangerous place, to say the least.

Perhaps, though, the lisowczyk rider is looking for something more than the enemy, something better than war and destruction, better than running and fighting, something about family, a wife, or a lover. Xavier Salomon suggests as much in the context of the rider representing all humanity, looking for something better especially in this new year after experiencing hardship and death in our own world and time. Maybe Rembrandt, after hearing again and again about the tribulations and wars of the Commonwealth decided to paint *The Polish Rider* looking back as a beacon of hope rather than of despair.

Think about it and enjoy *Cocktails with a Curator*. Please share if there is another idea on this painting.

Polish or Not?

The Intercollegiate Studies Institute (ISI) is a nonprofit educational organization whose mission is to "inspire college students to discover, embrace, and advance the principles and virtues that make America free and prosperous." You cannot beat that kind of guiding principle and the current president of ISI is Johnny Burtka. Johnny has been a guest commentator on several of the most popular talk shows recently.

He is a graduate from Hillsdale College with degrees in French and Christian Studies and earned a graduate degree in theology from La Faculté Jean Calvin in Aix-en-Provence, France. Johnny began his career at ISI, where he served as a development officer… He has been a Lincoln Fellow at the Claremont Institute and has participated in academic fellowships at Washington College and the Trinity Forum."

In an eMail, I asked him if he was Polish, and he answered, yes, and "Na Zdrowie!" To your health as well Johnny, keep espousing and promoting those great principles, and good luck going forward.

Another name spotted and quoted on television in recent months especially regarding the state of the COVID virus is Lidia Morawska. She is a "Professor at the Queensland University of Technology (QUT) in Brisbane, Australia, and the Director of the International Laboratory for Air Quality and Health."

Professor Morawska is a physicist, a graduate of the Jagiellonian University in Krakow, and is a consultant to the World Health Organization. Her specialty is the airborne dispersal of COVID-19 particles. A good paper to read on this subject authored by her and Donald K. Milton can be found online at (https://academic.oup.com/cid/article/71/9/2311/5867798).

Thought you might like to know. Laura Ingraham, host of *The Ingraham Angle* on Fox, was featured in a Pondering Pole column about television talk-show personalities that have a Polish background. Laura's mom is Anne Caroline Kozak whose parents were immigrants from Poland. Besides the *Angle*, Ingraham is a graduate of Dartmouth College, is a lawyer with a JD from the University of Virginia, and grew up in Glastonbury, Connecticut.

In her March 17, 2021, show, she had a piece about the state of teaching in public education and reminisced about the kinds of teachers she had back in Glastonbury. Names such as Markowicz, Kowaleski, and Bluchas were ones that caught my attention as she praised and thanked them for the impact they had on her life. "They were tough but fair, they were rigorous but acceptable." We are grateful for them as well.

I watched a lot of Masses during the previous year on the Eternal Word Television Network (EWTN). There is a lot of good programming on this channel and the current Chairman of the Board & Chief Executive Officer is Michael P. Warsaw. He has been with EWTN since 1991. Might be an obvious one but is Michael Warsaw, Polish or not?

We are breaking through to Spring (finally) and to a respite of the COVID (thankfully). For these two reasons, at least, life is good. Happy Constitution Day to all.

July-August 2021

"King of the Burin."

Folks will grouse unflinchingly about certain industries or agencies sometimes with merit but mostly without. The insurance industry, pharmaceutical companies, the airlines, and everyone's favorite, the United States Post Office. Criticism notwithstanding, I still use the Post Office for occasional shipping and utilize snail mail often. I will walk in to buy stamps from the clerk behind the counter and enjoy seeing what new special editions are being offered. I'm old fashioned in that way, I guess.

Talking about postage stamps, the Stamp Engravers Blogspot (https://stamp-engravers.blogspot.com/2019/03/biography-czeslaw-slania.html) makes this claim: "If there is one name synonymous with the art of stamp engraving, it must be that of Czeslaw Slania." Pronounced chesh'-wahv swah'-neeah, and according to Wikipedia, he was born in the town of Czeladz near Katowice, Poland, October 22, 1921. Besides being a prolific stamp engraver (having designed over 1000 stamps throughout his career), he also found work engraving banknotes and other documents. He garnered a spot in the *Guiness Book of World Records* for "the largest engraved stamp ever issued."

Since Slania is one of the best if not the best, it is important to know what is engraving and more specifically, stamp engraving. "Engraving is an art process where lines, dots, and dashes are cut into a soft metal plate with a tool called a burin. The engraving is done life size and in mirror reverse... Because engraving requires long years of study and extended apprenticeship, it is used for high security documents such as postage stamps and banknotes... Fine art productions usually require that only a few images are produced from each plate. In stamp production, many thousands, if not millions of impressions are made."

It is a complicated process and has seen several innovation iterations over the years. Engraving, in its various forms goes back hundreds, even thousands of years. One of the most famous engravers you know is Johannes Gutenberg, "printer and publisher who introduced printing to Europe with the printing press."

THE PONDERING POLE 2 2020–2023 and "BEST OF"

Czeslaw Slania began his life's work as a young boy impressing his classmates with his talent for drawing and subsequently used that ability during World War II to forge "identity cards and other documents for the Polish underground forces." When the war ended, he attended the Krakow Academy of Fine Arts specializing in "graphic techniques such as etching and copper engraving." That training and experience heightened his interest in engraving and jumpstarted his professional career working at the Polish Government Printing Works in 1950.

In 1956 because of the threat of increased oppression by the Soviet government, he moved to Sweden. There he found employment at the Swedish Post, the name for the Swedish postal service. At the Post, Slania honed his skills, tried new methods and techniques, and produced some of his best work. Like many of the great artists, he even added personal and humorous touches to some of his stamps.

> *Slania is known for his philatelic humor in that he often managed to include some personal or funny detail in his engravings. The earliest example of that is on the 1g40 value from the 1954 set marking the tenth anniversary of the Second republic, issued in Poland. The scene is a bookshop and Slania managed to incorporate the names of at least six people on a number of book covers: his mother, sister, cousin, niece and ex-wife, and the Chief of the Ministry of Post.*

As his fame and notoriety grew, so did requests by other national postal services for his service including Poland when the political climate began to thaw in the 1980s and 90s. The United States, Denmark, China, Great Britain, and the city-state of Monaco also commissioned him for stamp issues. He did all kinds of famous people, events, landscapes, and perhaps it was inevitable that Slania's "engraving of the old library building on a Faröe Islands stamp… was pronounced the most beautiful stamp in the world."

The superlatives on Czeslaw Slania specifically point to his greatness as a stamp engraver but the examples of his work I have seen makes me want to lump him in with all the great Polish artists and perhaps with all great artists. You can see many of his works on the Stamp Engraver Blogspot. Another possible source for research on Czeslaw Slania and Polish philately in general can be found on the Polonus Polish Philatelic Society website www.polonus.org.

Recommended, really?

Received a very nice letter from Irena Szewiola of the Polish Community Service Center of Van Nuys, California, regarding the continued inclusion of Art Spiegelman's graphic novel *Maus, A Survivor's Tale* (Pantheon Books, 1991) on the California Department of Education "Recommended Literature List" for grades 9-12. Irena has challenged *Maus* as appropriate to be on the list and I support that challenge as well.

The key word here is *appropriate* and without going into more detail for the reasons let me just say there are many better and more worthy books that could be used to teach and inform on the important subject of the Holocaust of World War II. Mrs. Szewiola has suggested, for instance, that *Children of Terror* by Inge Auerbacher and Bozenna Urbanowicz Gilbride (iUniverse, Incorporated, 2009) as better material for this subject.

If you agree on the Szewiola alternative to *Maus* or have other suggestions yourself, contact the California Department of Education, 1430 H Street, Sacramento, CA, 95814. Check out the recommended reading list in your own state for any inappropriate Polish entries. In your correspondence or contact, remember to be gentle, direct, and informed.

Polish or Not?

A tale of two Borowiaks, Tony and Jeff.

Tony Borowiak is one of the members of the American pop music group All4One. You might remember All4One's singles "I Swear" and "I Can Love You Like That" played frequently during the mid-1990s. The melodies are in my head right now. Great songs, Grammy winning group, and Borowiak is Polish and German on his father's side according to Ethnicelebs.com.

Jeff Borowiak was part of the mighty UCLA tennis program in the early 1970s that included Jimmy Connors and Haroom Rahim. Jeff was an NCAA Champion for the Bruins, is an accomplished musician, won five titles in his professional tennis career, two doubles titles, and, this is the one I find most fascinating, was also indirectly involved in the formation of the rock group Metallica. The story is Borowiak invested in his friend and Danish tennis player Torben Ulrich son's band called Lars Rocket, which later evolved into what we now know as Metallica. Jeff Borowiak, Polish or not?

THE PONDERING POLE 2   2020–2023 and "BEST OF"

Time Magazine puts out special edition issues periodically and one that I was given is *100 Photographs, The Most Influential Images of All Time*. Entries that make the final version of this kind of project are debatable of course but this one has many that would certainly be in my 100 as well. The cover shows the picture of the New York flat capped ironworkers eating their lunch while sitting on a beam from what looks like the 200th story of a skyscraper. That is one of my favorites and two of the other iconic shots have a Polish or maybe a Polish connection.

Dovima With Elephants "is one of the most famous fashion photographs of all time," and the subject of this picture by Richard Avedon, Dovima, "was one of the world's most famous models" in 1955. According to Wikipedia, she was born, Dorothy Virginia Margaret Juba, December 11, 1927, in Queens, New York. Her father was "Stanley Juba, a Polish-American policeman…"

The Betty Grable World War II pinup of the actress's backward glance over her right shoulder, in a bathing suit, and highlighting her "million-dollar legs," was shot by 20th Century Fox photographer Frank Powolny. The history I have read has him born in Austria to Czech parents Frank and Maria Powolny. The name Powolny means slow in Polish and while that is one connection to Polish, I am thinking there are others. Frank Powolny, Polish or not? Side note: Betty Grable, born Elizabeth Ruth Grable, St. Louis, Missouri.

If you watched the Hollywood Academy Awards this year, then you might have noticed the nominee for Art Director for the motion picture, *Promising Young Woman*, was Elizabeth "Liz" Kloczkowski. *Promising* was also nominated for picture of the year. That's huge. Another movie I thought was exceptionally good from 2018, also linked to the art direction of Liz Kloczkowski was *Under the Silver Lake*. Visit her website https://www.lizkloczkowski.com and you will see a very productive woman in several different areas of art with loads of talent. The name is Polish, but Elizabeth "Liz" Kloczkowski, originally from Massachusetts, graduate of Ithaca College, Ithaca, New York, Polish or not?

Happy Independence Day to all, be safe, not so much for fear of COVID but from celebrating too hard as the country gins up post COVID. It has been a wild spring around here anyway.

[56]

September 2021

About sausage "the way they used to" make it.

St. Peter: I see you wrote a book.

Pondering Pole: Yeah, I did. Whad'ya think?

St. Peter: I liked it. A few typos, grammatical errors, and some of the months are missing... but overall, it is full of information, optimism, and spirit and it is evident you had a wonderful group of interested and supportive people helping you and encouraging you along the way.

Pondering Pole: That's true. Thanks. Are you Polish, or not?

Made another trip (pilgrimage) to the Polka Fest in Pulaski, Wisconsin this past July and it was just great. Green Bay, the state of Wisconsin, the town of Pulaski, the Assumption Blessed Mary Virgin Church, the hopping polka music, dancing, food, and activities were all excellent. The festival brought loads of folks not only from the immediate area but from many other parts of the country as well.

My wife Sue and I hooked up with our friends Andy and Liz from California. If you weren't there this year, please try to go in 2022. I guess one thought that kept popping (hopping) into my mind was how much a part of Americana this festival is even while incorporating the "foreign" elements. Americana. It is us; I love it.

Soon after the Wisconsin trip a topic of conversation came up about how many long-time favorite establishments in the St. Louis metro area have closed and how many are still going strong. Coinciding with the latter, it happens that I was sent a story written by Stephen Jendrysik of The Republican newspaper out of Springfield, Massachusetts about the Blue Seal brand of kielbasa that is still being made in Chicopee, Massachusetts. Continuing for over 100 years, "Chicopee's flagship product is back in the stores. The

Chicopee Provision Co. survived a massive water line break, a factory reconstruction, and the COVID-19 crisis."

From the very beginning, it was the enterprising Stanislaw Sitarz who came up with the formula for making the Blue Seal kielbasa.

> *The pure pork, lean beef, and the delicate blend of spices, the nonpareil recipe was a stroke of pure genius, a new kind of sausage – lean, not greasy, catering to the American taste. It was a product to tempt the palate of all Western Massachusetts.*

In 1920, Sitarz went from a mere sausage shop and partnered with his brother Jacob and Bartomiej Partyka to create the Sitarz Manufacturing Co. Through a series of name changes, expansions, marketing and financial strategies, and additional investors, Situarz Manufacturing now called the Chicopee Provision Company, weathered depressions, recessions, a variety of competitors, and other challenges throughout the 30s, 40s, and 50s to "stay the course" and survive to this day still providing the same, first-rate, and delicious product. As summed up by Stephen Jendrysik,

> *How many times have you heard people remark that they don't make things the way they used to. There is a place they still do.*

Sto Lat to you Blue Seal and if you want to order some online here is the link https://bluesealkielbasa.com or check out the website for a store near you that carries it. I'm going to order some, and I hope you do too.

Another place they still "make things the way they used to."

I would be remiss if I did not mention our hometown sausage king, Piekutowski's European Style Sausage. I have mentioned them before and I'm having a plate of it now while finishing this column.

Piekutowski's, owned and operated by the family's fourth generation is 75 plus years in business and in St. Louis it is billed as "hand-made artisan" sausage because it is done with care and quality that cannot be replicated. That I believe. From their website,

There are ways to make our sausage faster or cheaper, but we are committed to using the finest cuts of meat, natural casings, quality spices and a slow hickory smoke. Because we are unwilling to sacrifice our heritage by cutting corners, our sausage has a difference you can taste.

If you would like to order some of the smoked kielbasa (and the krakowska is outstanding as well), the website is https://www.piekutowskis.com. My recipe for the best experience: take it out of the vacuum pack, peel off the casing, cut it in half inch sections, and boil in water for about ten-fifteen minutes. Drain and savor. None other than Saint John Paul II asked for some on his second visit to the city as pope. It is heavenly, trust me.

Polish or Not?

Demi Moore is an American actress who made it to the top despite what she went through in her youth. Suffice to say she had a rough childhood and adolescence but in her teen years it was a Polish connection that pushed her onto a path of stardom and fame. In an article on *The List* website (https://www.thelist.com/168106/the-untold-truth-of-demi-moore), when Demi was sixteen, she was inspired to become an actress from her neighbor at the time, Natasha Kinski.

Describing her neighbor, Moore added, "She had a real strong sense of who she was… I wanted to drink in. I wanted to learn what it was she had."

Though she is German by nationality, Natassia Kinski, according to ethnicelebs.com is Polish and German.

The academy missed it on this one for Best International Feature Film. I watched and recommend a Romance/Thriller movie I found on Amazon Prime, made in The Peoples Republic of China, called *Touch*. Released in 2020, it is about a western woman named Fei Fei (a translated name for Dorothy or Cindy?) who is married to a rich and important Chinese man. They throw lavish parties and live in a very large and exquisitely furnished home. After a strange meeting, she starts getting regular massages from a masseuse named Bai Yu who is blind. As described in the plot summary on imbd.com, "when they come together in an intense love affair, they find demons they've created implode in a clash of violent impulses."

You can make your own determination on the story leading up to and around the demons and impulses, but it was the acting, script, cinematography, and direction that was the most satisfying for me. The main character Fei Fei is played by Aleksandra Szczepanowska who also wrote, directed, and produced the film. She has "been the only western woman to make an independent film in the People's Republic of China." What delighted and captivated me most was seeing this European woman speaking in Chinese. Never seen anything like that.

In an interview from the Film Daily website (https://filmdaily.co/craft/aleksandra-szczepanowska-interview), Szczepanowska discusses her life before becoming a film maker, what inspired her to get into the film industry, what are her favorite directors, favorite movies, and what creative processes she employs. To get more insight on her, I recommend you read the whole interview.

Nowhere in that piece or anywhere else can I find what is her ethnicity or nationality. One of her favorite films is *Ida* (written and directed by Pawel Pawlikowski) and she enjoys listening to Jan Garbarek (well-known Norwegian jazz musician whose father is Polish). She has the look and name but is Aleksandra Szczepanowska, Polish or not?

This month especially, God bless all those that labor and apparently, we need even more folks laboring. For that matter, if you are young and energetic and looking for another career, something different, perhaps there is an old favorite establishment in your area with thoughts about turning over the keys to someone else. That someone can be you. Think about it.

October 2021

Saving all the "towns," "hills," and "villages."

Regarding "Poletown," the main topic for this issue of the Polish American Journal, let's start with a couple stories.

Back in the 80s, not long out of college, I worked for a medium-size regional airline headquartered in St. Louis and as a result was able to fly around domestically and internationally often and cheaply. During that same period, I discovered *Perspectives*, which some of you remember was a Polish American Educational and Cultural Bi-monthly periodical published by Polish-born Marta Korwin Rhodes out of Washington, D.C.

The mission of *Perspectives* was to heighten awareness through communication for Poles and others about overt bias and defamation aimed at Polonia in the United States. There was much of it then and I liked how Mrs. Rhodes chose to combat it. A workshop was held each year to discuss new issues, developments, and strategies. I attended several of them, met many great people, and subsequently my *perspective* on various things relating to Polonia changed.

While at the conference that occurred at the same time 11th hour appeals were being made to stop the destruction of Poletown (a Polish section of the city Detroit slated for government eminent domain), a young man from Detroit (didn't catch his name), reported with passion and pleading for those in attendance to contact company officials and politicians and join the fight to stop the destruction of the neighborhood. He was on the phone a lot and at times seemed frantic. He was amazing; I did nothing.

I'm sorry now I did not react with more interest but here is the other story with some irony. Before the Poletown tragedy, I had visited Poland and marveled at the medieval style cities and architecture. With that inspiration I created a proposal to develop, rebuild, and recreate a European village around St. Stanislaus Kostka Church in St. Louis that would complement and enhance its historic architecture and presence and utilize the vacant lots bordering the church property. I floated the idea to several individuals but to no avail. Perhaps it was too impractical or unappealing. Whatever the reason I filed it away for another day, which never came.

The lesson? Perhaps in the 80s there were still enough of us and our neighborhoods to go around and losing one to Detroit politicians and General Motors corporate muscle didn't seem like a big deal. Perhaps there was just too much on our own local plates and out with the old and in with new was in fashion for housing and corporate development. Now that our ethnic pie has gotten so much smaller what happens now to a Polish church or building in Detroit, Minneapolis, or Chicago becomes my fight.

While we still lose battles for individual structures and places, for comparisons sake, I am thinking about the bevy of Poletown like cultural and historical neighborhoods and areas in Chicago that are being preserved, naturally or by gentrification, from blight, flight, and destruction. One of those especially with a Polish connection is the Avondale neighborhood in the Northwest part of the city.

While much of it is mostly comprised of Hispanic residents, Avondale, along with Kosciuszko Park are "at the Northwestern edge of the Milwaukee Avenue 'Polish Corridor'- a contiguous stretch of Polish settlement which spanned this thoroughfare all the way from the Polonia Triangle at Milwaukee, Division and Ashland to Irving Park Road." Also called the "Polish Village" (or Jackowo), it is home to St. Hyacinth Basilica and St. Wenceslaus churches as well as many "Polish institutions that remain faithful to their traditions. With its offerings of sausage and Slavic pastries, Milwaukee Avenue between Central Park Avenue and Pulaski Road is the commercial heart of the neighborhood." Avondale is still there and holding.

Moving forward, it is important to remember that historical towns, hills, or villages and buildings are valuable because even if there is not one person living there or involved from the original group, the history and stability of the place is worth cherishing and preserving. That, at least, is my perspective on the legend of Poletown, or what is Avondale.

Polish or Not?

Jonas Piontek is a photographer from Germany who specializes in taking pictures of spectacular lightening shows and "dramatic pictures of landscapes in exceptional weather conditions" in all parts of the world. You can see his work on YouTube, Facebook, and visit his website http://jonaspiontek.com. Jonas is a German national and has the Polish name, but does he have a Polish connection, or not?

There is an artist that lives in Alton, Illinois (up the river from St. Louis) by the name of Christine Ilewski. "She has been the Visiting Artist for Liquitex for 20 years, bringing a materials and methods workshop to university campuses around the Midwest."

She mainly paints with acrylic, and her focus has shifted from human subjects to more recently landscapes with the mighty Mississippi as an inspiration and concept. Her studio overlooks the river. A worthy and heartrending undertaking and a direct answer to anyone that questions whether art has meaning is the Faces Not Forgotten project she started in 2013,

which uses portraits to memorialize young victims of gun violence… The families receive the original portrait, and a copy is used to create quilts that are exhibited nationally to raise awareness of this horrific loss.

That is powerful stuff, Christine has accomplished a lot, and you can view her work at https://www.chrisilewski.com. If you want to learn more about Faces Not Forgotten or to donate, visit http://facesnotforgotten.org.

I wrote about Blue Seal kielbasa last month based in the town of Chicopee, Massachusetts. To this day I remember the name and face of Mr. Ed Dobek of Chicopee who would also show up at the *Perspectives* conferences back in the 80s. What a delightful and friendly guy and I enjoyed seeing him and talking "Polish" with him. I loved the way he said "Chicopee" as he kept reminding me that is where he was from.

Happy Halloween and get out the sweaters. I saw one weather prediction for a very cold winter. Maybe we have turned the corner on the global warming. We shall see and have a bite-size Snickers for me.

November 2021

Anything you can do...

Like Annie Oakley, these Polish gals can outdo anyone especially if it comes to ballroom dancing and starting a financial services company. The first sharpshooter is Jowita Przystal and the second is Magdalena "Magda" Wierzycka. Not sure though how they would do riding horseback or singing in a Broadway musical.

Have you been waiting like I have for another beautiful female Polish hoofer to take over where Edyta Sliwinska of *Dancing with the Stars* left off? The wait is over. This year, the British version of *Dancing* called *Strictly Come Dancing* is adding Jowita Przystal as a member of the professional dancer corps. She comes to *Strictly Come Dancing* after finishing first in the 2020 British dance talent show, *The Greatest Dancer*, created by Simon Cowell.

Jowita was born August 22, 1994, in Krakow, Poland and started taking dance lessons when she was six years old. Her success and talent started to blossom after she hooked up with dance and life partner Michael Danilczuk who she met at a dance camp in Krakow in 2013. Danilczuk and Przystal won the Polish Open Latin Dance Championship in 2014 and in 2015 joined *Burn the Dance*, a live dance company "which has performed around the world, including on Broadway in New York City and the West End in London." They performed in several Broadway productions, then moved to London in 2019 to further their careers, and in 2020 they won the *Greatest Dancer* competition.

Both auditioned for *Strictly Come Dancing* but only Przystal was selected for the 2021 season. How does she feel about this new opportunity?

> *"This is my biggest dream come true. No words can describe how I feel right now. I'm still pinching myself to check if this is real, but I am beyond excited to be joining the Strictly Come Dancing family and I can't wait to give all of my heart and soul on that dance floor!"*

That's the spirit and we wish Pani Przystal all the luck! Here is hoping this will be a great first year in a long run with a wonderful television program.

I am not sure if Magda Wierzycka can dance but she certainly can pay for lessons if she needs them. At least one source has her as the richest woman in South Africa, but some are describing her worth at a measly billion. Poland has a number of men and women billionaires, and the Pondering Pole has written in the past about billionaire Polish self-made men such as Conrad Prebys and Ed Roski. Magda now joins that select club in the Polish woman billionaire column.

"One of South Africa's most successful businesswomen," Magdalena Franciszka "Magda" Wierzycka was born October 14, 1969, in Gliwice, Poland. When she was twelve and with the emergence of Solidarity and the subsequent social unrest the family moved to Austria "where they lived for a year in a Polish refugee camp… " In 1983 the family once again moved, this time to South Africa where she learned English and Afrikaans and attended Pretoria High School for Girls and the University of Cape Town.

Though her mother and father were doctors, Magda's career path leaned towards the financial services industry, and she found employment with insurance and fund management companies. Over time and after periods as director and CEO of various firms, she was able to orchestrate moves and deals cumulating in the "establishment of Sygnia Asset Management, a financial technology company."

> ***Wierzycka became the company's CEO in 2006. In a decade, she grew the company's assets from R2 billion to R162 billion which resulted in Sygnia becoming the second largest multi-management company in the country. On 14 October 2015, Sygnia was listed on the Johannesburg Stock Exchange.***

In case you were wondering, R2 and R162 mean that *revenues* for the company grew from 2 billion to 162 billion under her management. That is how you run a successful business and become a billionaire!!

Magda's hard work and persistence eventually paid off for her financially and she is a staunch fighter against corporate and political corruption. While I haven't seen the connection made public, perhaps it was the bad taste of Communism, corruption, and martial law in her country of birth that shaped

THE PONDERING POLE 2   2020–2023 and "BEST OF"

her feelings about corruption in her adopted country. What a super woman and a wonderful story.

Polish or Not?

Not sure if Johanna Maska can shoot straight or sing a tune but she is very savvy in the communications and political realm. Johanna hails from Galesburg, Illinois and became the Director of Press Advance in the Obama administration. That high profile job and her communications background subsequently catapulted her into jobs with the Los Angeles Times, the University of Southern California, and "she was senior vice president of communication and marketing for Karmic Labs."

Johanna Maska, Polish name, Polish face, but does she have a Polish connection, or not?

To counter all the nay-sayers out there for the Polish effort in World War II, simply stated, after the defeat of Poland, the Poles continued to fight or contributed for the duration in five theatres in World War II: the Eastern Front, the Western Front, North Africa, during the Battle for Britain, and, perhaps a stretch, the work Polish mathematicians did to crack the code for the German Enigma cypher machine. The code breaking was important in winning the war in the North Atlantic against Hitler's U-boats.

Watching a film on the fall of Norway in 1940 prompted me to do a little investigation of that history about a completely different part of Europe. To my surprise, a contingent of Polish soldiers fought under French command in what is called by the Germans as the Nordic Campaign. 533 French and Polish soldiers were killed or wounded in defense of Norway. Now I can add a sixth theatre, the Nordic.

Happy Thanksgiving Pondering Polers. Enjoy the holiday but remember to give thanks to someone or something. I will say, dziekuje bardzo, God bless, and good luck.

December 2021

"I owe everything to America."

Many of the shows I watch have current or former special forces people such as Navy SEALs or Army Rangers as analysts or commentators. The pullout in Afghanistan and the 20th anniversary of 9-11 were two recent examples. Since special ops are the best of the best, I'm always looking for a Polish name. Got my wish and more. Maybe an early Christmas present. It is the kind of story that fits well for our times and hopefully will lift your spirits as it did mine.

Appearing on *Unfiltered w/Dan Bongino* on Fox News in November, Thomas "Drago" Dzieran is a former Navy SEAL, born in Poland, and came to the United States in the 1980s to escape the Communist oppression that gave rise to the Solidarnosc' movement. His first job was an auto mechanic but later he became interested in serving in the U.S. military and aspired to becoming a SEAL even though at 32 he was several years past the normal age limit for admittance.

After completing rigorous testing, he was admitted to the program, served in the Iraq war, and stayed on with the force for 20 years as a member of SEAL Team 2, SEAL Team 4, and as an instructor at the Naval Special Warfare Center. He specialized as a Naval Special Warfare Lead Breacher performing "over 100 combat direct action missions" while in Iraq.

> *Everything I have, everything I own, I owe to America…*
> *Now I have a wonderful family, and everything I need*
> *to live, and most important – I am a free man.*

Dziekuje bardzo for your service Drago. You inspire us with your life and your heart.

THE PONDERING POLE 2   2020–2023 and "BEST OF"

"Well, you got it right."

In August of 2018 I read and wrote about a book called *The Clarinet Polka* (Thomas Dunne Books, St. Martin's Press, New York, 2002). The book was wonderful (but be advised there is adult language and content), and I deemed the author, Keith Maillard "amazing" for his knowledge of the "Polish soul" even though he was not Polish.

Every once in while I will page through my emails to make sure I have not missed something and I came across the one that I received from Keith at the time about the interest and purpose of the narrative in *Clarinet*, especially why the Polish part. In rereading that email, he told the moving story behind the story. Here is part of what he said, the fond feelings and his connection to Polonia.

> *Thanks for contacting me and for reading my book. In 2005* The Clarinet Polka *won The Polish American Historical Association's Creative Arts Prize, and my wife and I went down to Seattle to receive the prize. What I said to the historians on that night was that the prize should go to the people in the Polish community in my hometown, Wheeling, West Virginia, because I wrote the book to honor them and their culture, and that's true…*
>
> *After many years of research, I published the book. One of my Polish American friends called me up and said, "Well, you got it right." I was so relieved and happy to hear that. If people are still reading and enjoying the book, that makes me happy too. If you want to see the massive amount of research I did, turn to the back of the book and you will see much of it listed.*
>
> *In one of the standard academic texts, there's a letter that sticks in my mind. A Polish man in the 1890s is writing back to his family in Poland. He has come to America for the work. He writes something like this: "America is a terrible country. Here everyone has to be alone." But that's not true. When the Polish people settled in South Wheeling, they established the wonderful community that I still remember. They weren't lone isolated atoms,*

but interconnected and caring people. That's what the music was saying and what I could never forget.

Forgive me Keith for reading this in 2018 just as a confirmation on your sincerity and knowledge in writing *The Clarinet Polka*. While it is that, it is also a wonderful testament to something greater, something even many Polish Americans do not realize. You said it beautifully and we are humbled. Rereading it is one of the best Christmas cards I could receive. God bless you, thank you, and good luck.

Polish or Not?

Jacques Pepin, "French-born American chef, author, culinary educator, television personality, and artist," is one of my most favorite TV chef personalities. Love watching him cook, explain how he is cooking, and just talking about cooking and life in general. Now I have discovered another "side" to Chef Pepin's personality and greatness. That other part is Jean-Claude Szurdak.

Jean-Claude Szurdak was the "long time cooking partner" of Jacques and a best friend for over 50 years. As one reporter said of the relationship between Jacques and Jean-Claude (https://www.foodandwine.com/chefs/jacques-pepins-buddy-system), they

are like brothers, or like a long-married couple. Except that in my experience no brothers or spouses get along so well. "Before we were married, before children, before accidents, before everything, we were already together, cooking in the same way," Jacques says. "We are forged from the same material."

Szurdak owned and managed a high-end catering company in New York City for over 20 years, taught at the Boston University Culinary Arts school, has been a frequent guest for many of Pepin's projects over the years, and loved by his students and patrons alike. Polish looking name, but is Jean-Claude Szurdak, Polish or not?

Szurdak, and another high-profile and successful person is Chris Markowski, the "Watchdog on Wallstreet." From his website https://watchdogonwallstreet.com,

THE PONDERING POLE 2   2020–2023 and "BEST OF"

For 20 years, savvy, independent retirement savers and individual investors have tuned into our radio show and now our popular podcast, "The Watchdog on Wall Street" for a raw, unfiltered take on the intersection of Wall Street and the Beltway.

Watchdog is billed as "the longest running financial program in the country" and represents the pinnacle in a career for Markowski as an author, investment banker, and equity analyst, all under the umbrella of helping the consumer make good and sound decisions regarding their financial health.

Along with the *Watchdog* radio show and podcast, Chris is Partner and Advisor with Markowski Investments, Inc. (along with his brothers Matt and Michael), and has appeared on Fox Business, CNN, Newsmax, and other cable networks. You can read more about the company at https://minvest.com. Polish name, but Chris Markowski, Polish or not?

At Christmas, especially, remember that we do belong to that "wonderful community" of people and believers. Cherish it and Wesolych Swiat Bozego Narodzenia to you and your family.

IV
2022

January 2022

~~Star Trek~~ *Polonia: The next generation.*

"I think it will be a name that will go down in galactic history… "

Captain James Kirk, starship USS Enterprise

My daughters and I have this thing where we let each other know about notable events in space such as what occurred on November 19th, 2021, where the longest *partial* (covered about 99% of the moon's disk) lunar eclipse happened since the year 1440. The next longest *total* lunar eclipse is coming November 8, 2022. Mark your calendar and get ready to wake up at 3:00 am to look (and maybe howl) at the moon.

Now for a big coincidence (or just a coincidence; there are no big or small coincidences, Rava, April 11, 1991, episode of *Seinfeld*), the next day I was looking for a particular Polish name which led to "Polish Names in Space" found in Wikipedia. Polish Names in Wiki is a listing of space objects and features named after Polish people. There are other nationalities you can plug in the search bar (Latvian Names in Space, Uruguay Names, and Thai) but I was excited to see what this was all about for the Polish.

Many of the names are famous and familiar such as Chopin (Moon crater), Copernicus (Martian crater), and Mickiewicz (a crater on Mercury). Some are simply common Polish names like Wanda, Jadwiga, Janina, and Zosia, all women names for craters on Venus, a planet named after a woman. Those that most interested me were of people and things named after astronomers and references I was not aware. Here are examples of those.

Moon, Arminski crater. Franciszek Arminski, born 1789, was a Polish astronomer, professor, and eventually rector of the newly founded Warsaw University in 1812. There he created in 1825 an observatory complete with a "heliometer for measuring the Sun, a comet-finder, and three clocks made by 'Gugenmus of Warsaw.'"

Moon, Kepinski crater. "In 1979, the International Astronomical Union named the Kepinski crater on the moon after Felicjan Kepinski." This Polish astronomer, professor, and editor was consumed with space study and research throughout his life and earned degrees from various European universities in philosophy, mathematics, and astronomy.

Asteroid, Iwanowska 198820. Born September 2, 1905, in Wilno, Wilhemina Iwanowska was an astronomer and "was a pioneer of astrophysics in Polish science." Notable research includes discovering "a new scale of distance in the universe" and for her characterization of "stellar super giants based on the analysis of their spectral features." She was awarded honorary degrees at the University of Winnipeg, Canada, University of Leicester, England, and at Torun University in Poland.

Exoplanet, Pirx. Of all the famous sci-fi writers in history, Poland has produced at least one of the greatest in Stanislaw Lem. Pirx is an exoplanet "named during the NameExoWorlds campaign by Poland." "Pilot" Pirx is a fictional character appearing in Lem's 1979 *Tales of Pirx the Pilot*, and in his 1982 work *More Tales of Pirx the Pilot*.

Check out the entry in Wiki for other naming. The truth is Poland has a long history in the study of the heavens and like the endless frontier of space, there is still so much more to learn. Live long and keep learning.

Polish or Not?

First things, I received an email from Chris Markowski, the "Wallstreet Watchdog," unfortunately after submitting my December 2021 article. The answer to the Markowski "Polish or not?" question for December is dad is Polish, and mom is Italian. Na Zdrowie!, keep up the excellent work, and we are happy to have you in the family Chris!!

There are a number of them out there, but Mina Starsiak Hawk is another gal hosting a home renovation show. Along with her mother Karen E. Laine, she is the star of the HGTV's *Good Bones*. *Bones* has run for six seasons and the premise is to create "green spaces whenever possible and incorporating work by local artists and craftsman to put a personal touch on the homes." Her father is Casey (Casimir?) Starsiak, an orthopedic surgeon, and she has a half-brother named Tad (Tadeusz?). Mina Starsiak Hawk, Polish or not?

Do you remember a movie from the 70s called *Vanishing Point*? The main character played by Barry Newman is a guy named Kowalski (no first name), who is a "dissatisfied ex-policeman and race driver delivering a souped-up car cross country to California while high on speed…"

Thin plot but it worked for me (Steven Spielberg and Quentin Tarantino liked it as well), and the film garnered a cult following and did very well at the box-office for the producers. In 1997 the hard rock band Primal Scream made an album by the same name. It is "meant to be an alternate soundtrack to the film." One of the songs on the album is "Kowalski." I listened to Primal's Kowalski and… well, you can judge for yourself. It is one of their "hits."

"Python" Joe Wasilewski is a legendary character in the Florida Everglades for his tenacious quest to rid this ecosystem of the non-native Burmese python species.

You don't want to be bitten by a python." Joe tells people. "They aren't venomous, but they have powerful jaws and long, curved teeth meant to hold on. When one grabs you, your impulse is to yank your hand away. But that tears muscle and flesh. What I've learned is patience. If I make a mistake and one bites me, you just have to stand there and wait. Sometimes five minutes go by before it lets go."

Nice advice from Joe on your next trip to South Florida. You can read more about Joe Wasilewski, also known as the "snake man," in various articles online, but I could not verify if he is, Polish or not?

When someone is "influential" in the creation, design, discovery, or development of something, then that person is important. Leonard Chess, born Lejzor Szmuel Czyz, March 12, 1917, to Polish-Jewish parents in the town of Motal, Poland, was "influential in the development of electric blues, Chicago blues, and rock and roll." The last one is the subject of a documentary on Prime called, *The Howlin' Wolf Story*. Leonard Chess founded Chess Records and produced recordings for such famous musical stars such as Chester Arthur Burnett (a.k.a. Howlin' Wolf), Muddy Waters, Bo Diddley, Chuck Berry, Etta James, Fontella Bass, among others.

From Wiki, "Leonard Chess was the dynamo behind Chess Records, the label that, along with Atlantic and Sun, has come to epitomize the independent record business…" I think we owe a debt of gratitude to Leonard Chess primarily for the promotion and preservation of unique and prodigious musical talent and genres. Whether he realized it or not, he truly was part of the "birth of rock and roll."

Happy New Year, God bless, and good luck in 2022. This will be the greatest year ever for you. Believe it.

February 2022

Lodz you believe it.

A long time ago in a class at the local Junior College I heard an Eastern European accent from one of the students and asked the young woman, what country and what city? She was in fact Polish and grew up in Lodz (pronounced like "wood" only replace the "d" with a soft "j" as in the word judge - woohj). I also asked her what her professional background was, and she replied – Nuclear Physicist. Say that again?

One of my spotters passed on the name Arthur Szyk to me as one who is successful and interesting and has a Polish connection. Like the Nuclear Physicist, he was born in Poland in the city of Lodz, June 16, 1894. At an early age he was accepted at the Academie Julian, a distinguished and important art school in Paris. He returned to Poland in 1913 and continued his studies at the Krakow Academy of the Arts. Szyk was a participant in both World War I and the Polish-Soviet War both militarily and using his talents as an artist.

During the inter-war period, Szyk found work and prominence as an artist and book illustrator and continued doing illustrations throughout the 20s and 30s into the second World War and beyond, gaining more notoriety. The style of his work is "much like the illuminated manuscripts of the 16th century," with "intricate borders, decorated initials, and patterns to bring the pages to life." The pieces are done in watercolor and gouache ("a technique of painting with opaque watercolors prepared with gum") and whether the subject was Hitler, Pulaski, or the pasha of Marrakech, the figures jump out in an exaggerated and bold way. You are forced to look, and I see many influences from the past and to future artists in his work.

You can find more about him on the website https://www.szyk.com. Truly an amazing man who created beautiful and important art. While I was at it though, consider either that Arthur Szyk had great genes or maybe it was the vibe in Lodz that rubbed off on him. Nuclear Physicist and renowned artist?

Checking out Lodz, the city, there are a lot of important and amazing people that came from that place. People like Arthur Rubenstein, Jerzy Kozinski, Andrzej Bartkowiak, Jacob Bronowski, Max Factor, Roman Polanski, and Wladyslaw Reymont. The mayor, a woman, is Hanna Zdnowska and Marian P. Opala, who fought for Poland in World War II, and later sat on the Supreme Court for the state of Oklahoma in the United States. I want to go there, drink the water, and see in person what makes these Lodzians tick.

Polish or Not?

As a father to two girls, it was natural for me to track the Disney movies throughout the years and then all the other "kid" films produced along with them. I even owned Disney stock in the past and now with grandchildren, I am still bullish on the shows. All along I was hoping for a Polish cast of characters or at the least a plot or theme built around Eastern Europeans. *Moana* only with Tadziu and Danuta.

Count Mike Wazowski (voice by Billy Crystal), who is the main character in the 2013 *Monsters University* as one and that is cool. I am sure there are others, but it was a great delight to watch *Ron's Gone Wrong*, a 2021 computer-animated production of Locksmith Animation with the Pudowski family taking the lead roles. *Ron's* is set in the year 2042 and concerns Barney Pudowski's relationship with his "B-bot," a robot designed to "help make friends." Graham Pudowski is Barney's dad and thick-accented Polish immigrant grandma Donka lives with them substituting for mom who is non-existent in the story.

According to one of the writers, Peter Baynham, the original inspiration for Donka was his grandmother who "used to give me raw pork sausages as a kid and crazy things, and she'd boil a cow's tongue in the kitchen." Not sure whether Baynham's grandmother was Polish or whether her cooking skills alone were the "inspiration" for Donka. Baynham was a co-writer, along with Sacha Baron Cohen for the film *Borat: Cultural Learnings of America for Make Benefit Glorious Nation of Kazakhstan*.

The raw pork sausages and *Borat* connection will probably make you think the Pudowski's portrayal has to be a negative, but I did not see that. The only thing I thought was ridiculous was the look and mannerisms of Donka which were more consistent with an early 19th or 20th century Polish village woman rather for someone in the year 2042. (Hollywood people still cannot believe that

Poland is not a country full of peasants.) She is, however, a lovable character, and as Sarah Smith, who co-wrote *Ron's* with Baynham, describes her as "that kind of brilliant matriarch who will kill a chicken and mend the car," and one who is "warm and sympathetic."

Perhaps co-writer Smith and Donka's voice actor Olivia Colman saved us from any deep-seated derogation that Baynham might have been inclined but we are grateful whatever the case. Unless I need to study the movie much closer or missed something, I feel this picture will be a fun and positive experience for you and your children. Do let me know what you think.

How about Polish movie trivia? *The Great Escape* produced in 1963 is one of the classics in American film history. It is rich with great actors in lead and supporting roles such as Steve McQueen, James Garner, and Richard Attenborough. Charles Bronson, of Polish descent, plays the character Danny Welinski, a Polish pilot flying with the English Royal Air Force (RAF). He plays the "tunnel king" but at this point in his incarceration is suffering from claustrophobia.

The action revolves around how American and British prisoners at Stalag Luft III, a German prisoner of war camp for Allied airmen and run by the Luftwaffe work together to dig tunnels, escape, and interrupt and inhibit operations for the German war effort as they try to recapture them. The problem is it didn't happen like that. The airman primarily involved in *The Great Escape* belonged to the British Commonwealth or were their allies as of March 24, 1944, when the real escape occurred. In fact, a segment of the pilots in the camp were Polish nationals shot down flying for the RAF.

The denouement from the 1963 movie and the actual event of March 1944 (as described in the book by the same name by Australian writer Paul Brickhill) is when 76 men go through the tunnel and are dispersed throughout Europe fleeing from the Gestapo agents assigned to round them up. On Hitler's orders, 48 of those recaptured were shot. Of the 48, 20 were British, 6 Canadian, 6 Polish, and the rest from other countries. The second highest count of the murdered were Poles. The next time you watch the 1963 American version of the movie, keep this in mind.

Lodz, the city, was interesting for its history and relevance and that was a nice "bonus." Happy Valentine's Day to all the and Pondering Poles readers out there. Spread the love.

March 2022

Trains, Planes, and... Well, just trains.

Before getting to the main topic, here are a couple of interesting items to ponder.

At the end of an interview in the January/February 2022 AARP Bulletin newspaper, Mel Brooks, age 95, the famous comedian, writer, actor, and director was asked, "What's your secret, Mel? How have you sustained such a high level of creativity throughout your life?" His answer, "I'd say stuffed cabbage has kept me going. I love it… " Smacznego Mel!

While eating stuffed cabbage, I watched a remarkable movie on Netflix called *Passing*, starring Tessa Thompson and Ruth Negga. The story is about two African American women who grew up together through high school, went separate ways, and then reconnected again later in life. The setting is 1920s New York. Irene, "Ree-nee," lives in Harlem with her physician husband and Claire is married to a white man and is "passing" for Caucasian. Claire's husband does not know she is African American. At one point, Claire tells Irene, "I want so much to be around Negroes again. Talk with them, hear them laugh. I've almost forgotten it… " Like Claire, are you "passing," longing for the cultural experience that you grew up with, are familiar with?

Something I grew up with and I think most male baby boomers did have experience with was model trains. Like me, some of my relatives, and friends just had a basic circle or oval set up (usually under the Christmas tree) but there were others that really got into it (or their dads really got into it) and had more elaborate displays and intricate track layouts. I marveled at theirs, those at the hobby shops, or at the special events for department stores. Lionel and HO were the most popular brands.

So, if this memory spurs you to get out and play with the old Lionel or HO train set, great, or if you happen to be in Moosic, Pennsylvania, you absolutely must stop in the Grzyboski's Train Store. A saying from this family-run business is "Happy Railroading" and for over 30 years they have been offering "quality products and a growing knowledge of the ever-changing technology in modern era trains."

In reading the story about this "mom and pop" store (Joe Jr. and Theresa Grzyboski), several things stand out. It truly is family oriented with children, in-laws, and even third generation Grzyboskis involved in operations, shipping, customer service, and sales. They do over 25 model train shows every year and their new location in Moosic "is styled after an old fashion train station with a modern warehouse facility attached." ScotchBuilt, Inc., the contractor who built the new store won the 2007 Master Builder Award for the construction of the building. Grzyboski's is one of Lionel's Top 10 Dealers.

If you cannot visit in person, you can see information about the store and the trains and accessories for purchase online at https://www.grzyboskitrains.com. Happy Railroading!

Railway Engineers from Poland.

From model trains to the kind that carry real people, coal, or iron ore, and were sometimes prey to Jesse James, here are a couple of famous Polish rail engineers, the kind that design them rather than drive them.

Polish railway engineers were noteworthy in many parts of the world but one that is famous near and within his own country is Stanislaw Kierbedz. Born March 10, 1810, into a Polish family from Lithuania, he studied mathematics and physics at the University of Vilinius (Wilno). In 1831, Kierbedz obtained a degree in St. Pertersburg, Russia, from the Institute of the Corps of Engineers Communications. From 1834 to 1849 he visited various schools and universities throughout Europe and taught engineering at the Institute of Mining and the Warsaw School of Engineers as well as the St. Petersburg Institute of the Corps of Engineers.

After his tenure as a teacher, he found employment as an engineer and some of his biggest projects were the construction of the St. Petersburg-Warsaw Railway in 1852, the Kierbedz bridge in Warsaw in 1862, the construction in 1856-57 of the St. Petersburg-Peterhof Railway, and in 1858 "was a member of the Head Council of Railways and Public Buildings Direction." He designed and supervised "dozens" of bridges and railway lines.

Ernest Adam Malinowski found fame and fulfillment on the other side of the globe. Born January 5, 1818, in the city of Seweryny in the Wolyn region he "was a Polish civil engineer best known for constructing the world's highest railway at the time, the Ferrovias Central, in the Peruvian Andes between 1871-1876." Also referred to as the Transandean Railway, it became the paramount project of his life even though he did not live to see its completion.

In his youth, because his family became embroiled in the November Uprising of 1830-1831, Ernest, his father, and his brother moved to Paris, France to avoid persecution from the Russian government. It was in Paris that he studied at Ecole Polytechnique and Ecole des Ponts et Chaussees and after graduating found employment in Algeria and France. Eventually he "signed a contract with a representative of the Peruvian government and moved to that country."

The work he was assigned in Peru gave him the opportunity to hone his skills as an engineer and in 1866, Kosciuszko-like, allowed him to build fortifications and even join in the fighting during Peru's war with Spain. After the conflict, Malinowski began building a number of railway lines and in 1871 began work on the Transandean Railway.

> *The project required a titanic amount of work. The Transandean Railway was the subject of increasing publicity in the world – not only because it climbed to previously inaccessible heights (almost 5,000 metres above sea level), but also because of the technological miracle that it represented.*

Ernest Malinowski lived an incredible life, was recognized as a Polish and Peruvian national hero, and can be considered one of the world's great railway engineers. For more information on his life and work, consult the website, Institut De Republica (https://iderepublica.pl/en/the-institute).

Polish or Not?

This one should go under the category of "Polish Just as Good or Better" and certainly is information you need to know. The Polish army in World War II had their own set of tanks used against the Germans and Russians in 1939. The best one was a modified version of the British Vickers 6-ton called the 7 TP, "7" representing the amount, "T" for tonnage, and "P" for Polish. Prior to the war, the Poles did quite a bit of research and development on tank weaponry and the 7 TP was the best they had at the start of the war.

The problem was the number of 7 TPs built, trained, and in use for the war. The Germans had a 4 to 1 advantage in tanks and only a portion of the Polish compliment were the 7 TP. However, according to Wikipedia, it was "… technically superior to any of the German light tanks of the era." For all the talk about the German Panzers, etc., the Poles claimed at least one superior tank.

One other bit of Polish tank trivia you can take to the bank is that the 7 TP was equipped with the Gundlach tank periscope, a "revolutionary invention by Polish engineer Rudolf Gundlach" and "manufactured for Polish 7 TP tanks from the end of 1935…" Not only was this periscope "used in almost all tanks of WWII, including the British Crusader, Churchill, Valentine, and Cromwell and the American M4 Sherman," but after the defeat of Poland, the Germans and Russian "borrowed" the technology for use with existing and new versions of their tanks. Also remember the Poles and their 7 TP tank were not allowed to walk in the victory parade in London.

Rachel Anne Zegler, who plays Maria in the Steven Spielberg 2021 remake of *West Side Story* has a father who is mostly Polish (Zimnicki, Porowski, and Lakowski from ethnicelebs.com) with a quarter mix of German and Italian. Her mom is from the country of Columbia. Can the Spielberg version be better than the original? We shall see.

Happy Pulaski Day and hopefully spring is around the corner. Oh, and Happy Railroading.

April 2022

From lab rat to CEO.

For eleven years I worked in IT (Information Technology) at a hospital. We managed the computer service for the administrators and staff and the job I had gave me the opportunity to interact with each of the hospital departments. Funny thing, they all had their own kind of personality. The OR (Operating Room/Surgery Department) was the Irish clan (Meg, Colleen, Rosalee, Brian), Respiratory Therapy had a sixties laidback vibe, and the Emergency Room had Hawkeye and Trapper John. These two guys weren't wild and crazy, but they were two tall lovable guys with a notable presence. Laboratory techs were super serious, and they emphasized procedure and exactness. I loved working with all the "cultures" within the hospital and especially with the Lab folks.

Quest Diagnostics is an American clinical lab company that also has operations in Puerto Rico, Mexico, and Brazil, and "maintains collaborative agreements with various hospitals and clinics across the globe." It is a Fortune 500 company with 48,000 employees and in 2021 posted over $10 billion in revenues. In 2012, Stephen Rusckowski was appointed President and CEO of the company.

Stephen "Steve" Rusckowski was born in Torrington, Connecticut in 1956 and is a graduate of St. Mary's grade school. His mother, Veronica is the daughter of Joseph Staszkowski who was born in Przewronte, Poland in 1890. He has a degree in Mechanical Engineering from Worcester Polytechnic Institute (WPI) and a Master of Science degree in Management from the Massachusetts Institute of Technology's Sloan School of Management. He has the reputation as a hard worker and though coming from a "humble background," education was the foundation for lifelong learning and success in his family. From the WPI website Fall 2020 (https://wp.wpi.edu/journal/articles/stephen-rusckowski-79),

> *"Engineering was the path I thought would work for me," he says. "And WPI had a good reputation in my town."*

While his sister was a scientist, his older brother was an engineer, and his cousin a WPI grad. With a generous financial aid package, and his parents' encouragement of higher ed, WPI was his decision in the end... But that was part of the learning process, and a helpful part of those four years was to figure out, in a clear and definitive way, what you needed to do to become a professional engineer.

After college, Steve Rusckowski began his career at The Proctor & Gamble Company assuming several management positions and even though his background was in engineering, in 1984 he was hired on at Hewlett-Packard Company in their medical division. In 1999 he became Senior Vice President and GM of the Healthcare Systems Group. He became CEO of Phillips Healthcare in 2005 until 2012 when he left to join Quest Diagnostics.

In his time as chief executive, Rusckowski led Quest from a stagnant state to one of exponential growth. He did so by prioritizing the company's advanced diagnostics and consumer testing segments and its relationships with insurers and healthcare providers, and by building out Quest's reach through a total of 41 acquisitions. These efforts culminated in 2021 with the company's strongest financial performance to date. It registered total revenues of $10.8 billion, representing not only a 14.3% increase from 2020, but an almost 50% improvement over the $7.4 billion Quest posted in 2012, his first year in office (https://biotech-today.com/quest-ceo-rusckowski-to-step-down-after-a-decade-following-record-setting-2021).

The COVID pandemic has been a challenge on how Quest would respond and Rusckowski was a consultant to Vice President Mike Pence's Coronavirus Task Force.

"It's been a wild ride," he says of his time since that early March phone call. The pandemic, however, has highlighted exactly what Rusckowski has championed all along—the importance of low-cost, high-accuracy diagnostic tests... "It goes back to that simple notion that diagnostic tests are a very small fraction of cost," he says, "but are such an important part of healthcare."

Stephen Rusckowski will turn over the reins in May of 2022 but will remain as executive director on the Quest Board of Directors until March of 2023. Excellent job and good luck to the President, CEO, and Executive Director of a giant clinical lab company which is now worth over $15 billion. Not bad for the lab rat from Torrington.

Polish or Not?

Married to the Pole is information you need to know about Anna Anka. I always wondered if "Anka" was Polish or another Eastern European extraction, but Paul Anka, the great Canadian singer, songwriter, and actor is Lebanese. However, the woman he was married to from 2008-2010 was Anna Aberg, born Danuta Anna Kolokiejska. She was adopted by a Swedish couple at age three and grew up in Sweden. She is a model, actress, and writer and appeared in season 1 of *Svenska Hollywoodfuar*, Swedish Hollywoood Wives.

Say cheese! The Polish American Journal has featured this subject in the past and though I had never heard of it or tasted it, there is a famous Polish cheese called Oscypek. Oscypek per the *Key to Poland* website (https://keytopoland.com/post/oscypek-traditional-polish-highland-cheese) is a "traditional smoked cheese made of salted sheep milk hailing from the highland Tatra Podhale region of Poland."

Oscypek is made from milk from a specific breed of sheep in the Polish highlands, is refined and enhanced through an intricate process, placed in molds called oscypiorka, and then smoked. "In 2008, this cheese was protected under the EU's Protected Designation of Origin certification which means when you buy it you need to make sure you are getting the "authentic thing." Yes, the real deal and though I am lactose intolerant, I hope someday to try it. *Key to* is an excellent source to read more about this Polish made cheese.

May-June 2022

In pursuit of a cure.

Okay, this one hit close to home. It is special because my mother suffers from Alzheimer's.

In February of this year, the American science community lost one of its major "research pioneers" with the death of John Q. Trojanowski. Born December 17, 1946, in Bridgeport, Connecticut, he was an academic research neuroscientist and "one of the world's leading authorities on abnormally folded proteins that damage the brain" resulting in the onset of Alzheimer's disease, Parkinson's, or Amyotrophic Lateral Sclerosis (ALS).

John was the son of Maurice Trojanowski, an Air Force officer, and spent much of his childhood moving from base to base as a military kid. He was a graduate of King's College in Wilkes-Barre, Pennsylvania and received a combined MD-PhD from Tufts University in Massachusetts. While doing his residency at Massachusetts General Hospital he met his future wife Virginia Man-Yee Lee, MBA, PhD. "She was a researcher at Boston Children's Hospital. They married in 1979 and worked as researchers at the University of Pennsylvania for the rest of his life."

The work that he did to understand "how the brain functions" was extraordinary. He wrote more than 500 scientific papers, "mentored many doctoral fellows who went on to become leading professors at major medical schools," and the list of awards he received includes the First Pioneer Award from the Alzheimer's Association (1998-2003), an Award for Meritorious Contributions to Neuropathology from the American Association of Neuropathologists (June 2015), and the Alzheimer's Association Lifetime Achievement Award in Alzheimer's Disease Research (July 2018). "His colleagues at the University of Pennsylvania said that his scientific contributions were 'phenomenal.'"

Not only did Trojanowski work in the lab for solutions to neurodegenerative diseases, but he was also an advocate for a healthy lifestyle and how it can make a difference in preventing them. This included producing two films to educate the public on "what is needed to cure and/or prevent disorders like Alzheimer's Disease." We need a million more like John Trojanowski and his wife, Virginia. Though he is no longer with us, his work will continue to bring us closer to ending the scourge of diseases such as Alzheimer's, Parkinson's, and ALS.

Polish or Not?

I'm always wondering about the "expert" on the cable talk shows and Luke Rosiak was one such guest commentator recently. Luke has authored an important book on a salient topic for our times - education. The book is *Race to the Bottom: Uncovering the Secret Forces Destroying American Public Education* (Broadside Books, March 2022) and it examines why American kids are not learning as well as they should be and the agendas and forces that are driving this downward trend. I have the book and am ready to read it.

Luke's regular job is "an investigative reporter for the Daily Caller News Foundation," he was an investigator for the Senate Homeland Security and Government Affairs Committee, and has held positions at the *Sunlight Foundation*, the *Washington Post*, the *Washington Times*, and the *Washington Examiner*. As a topper, in an email from Luke, "I visited Warsaw once about ten years ago to see the land of my heritage." His is on a career path we need to track, and we wish him wszystkiego najlepszego. All the best!

You might wonder where certain words got their origin. This month's sorrowful word is Genocide, and it is the combination of the Greek word "genos," race or tribe, and a derivative from Latin "cide," meaning "killer" or "act of killing." "In 1944, Raphael Lemkin coined the term *genocide*…"

Raphael "Rafal" Lemkin was born June 24, 1900, in the town of Bezwodne, in what is now Belarus but grew up in a Polish-Jewish family on a large farm near Wolkowysk. His father tended the farm, and his mother was an artist, linguist, and taught their children from home. Lemkin's interest in "Genocide" began as a young man when he learned about various mass killings throughout history and then later as a lawyer, he became intrigued with the Armenian mass killings of 1915-1917, wondering why there was no legal recourse or retribution for the perpetrators of that crime.

From that point onward, throughout the Second World War, and beyond he worked to ratify the international Genocide Convention treaty which "criminalizes genocide and obligates state parties to enforce its prohibition." It was finally adopted by the United Nations General Assembly on December 9, 1948. It could not be more fitting that a person of Polish and Jewish background would study and devise a word for one of humanities most dreaded acts.

This month we feature Nadia Tereszkiewicz, a new and bright "French-Finnish actor and dancer with Polish heritage."

I discovered Nadia from her performance in *Only the Animals* (she plays the character Marion), an excellent 2019 French mystery film. According to the online French magazine, *Crash*, Tereszkiewicz is one of a handful of actors who "form the vanguard of a portfolio dedicated to the new faces of French film," and "whose charismatic performances have electrified the big screen in recent years."

Check out her work on imdb.com, learn more about her in *Ten Facts About Nadia Tereszkiewicz* (https://www.characterswiki.net/13210/nadia-tereszkiewicz-facts-to-know-about-possessions-actress), and on *Crash*, in an interview with Armelle Leturcq (https://www.crash.fr/a-meeting-with-nadia-tereszkiewicz).

The horrors of war!! Fox News mourned the death of one of their admired and beloved colleagues, 55-year-old cameraman Pierre Zakrzewski, who was killed March 14, 2022, when he and Ukrainian journalist Sasha Kuvshynova, who was also killed, came under fire in the town of Horenka, near Kyiv.

Zakrzewski was described as brave, professional, profoundly committed to telling the story, and "he did it all under immense pressure with tremendous skill." Pierre's father was Polish and his mother French. He was a great guy and will be missed.

Received a kind email from Paula from Toledo, Ohio, which included her "experience" with Oscypek cheese, mentioned in last month's Pondering Pole. She talked about her trips to Poland in the 80's and 90's and how they would always include a visit to Zakopane. A woman who had a business "hawking her cheese" to Dunajec raft riders approached the group. As Paula tells it:

THE PONDERING POLE 2   2020–2023 and "BEST OF"

… our guide Gregory (also in the picture) took a sample slice and proclaimed it was: "Smaczny!" and he suggested I take one too. In my opinion – that taste was good for a LONG time.

That is funny and I guess is consistent with the assessment that many of our Polish foods can be described as hearty, earthy, or robust. Dziekuje bardzo to you Paula for sharing and now I really cannot wait to try it!!

July-August 2022

MAUS no more?

*F*irst, sad news, my dear mother, Audrey Mueller passed away June 7, 2022. She lived life to the fullest and was a true Polonian. We will miss her, but I am happy, as it was said, that she has been released from her miserable condition. Say a prayer for my stepfather Ron Mueller and the Poniewaz and Lamczyk families. Na zdrowie Aud! I love you, I will always think of you, and I will drink a perfect Manhattan in your honor, often.

The Catholic League for Religious and Civil Rights (The Catholic League) "is the nation's largest Catholic civil rights organization. It defends individual Catholics and the institutional Church against defamation and discrimination." The Catholic League is similar to the NAACP for Blacks, or the Anti-Defamation League (ADL) for Jews, or the Polish American Congress for the Poles. We need these organizations to protect and defend those outside the mainstream when the psychotic disorders of some humans and societies get out of hand.

In The League's May 2022 newsletter *Catalyst* came a report that more than 200 leaders in Polonia signed and delivered a letter to members of Congress asking that the cartoon book *MAUS*, about a Holocaust experience during World War II, be "discontinued in the schools."

> **The best-selling graphic novel, MAUS, by Art Spiegelman, which is targeted at children, features illustrations that are outrageous and needlessly offensive. But it is the lies, and vicious insults hurled at Poles, that merit the most serious condemnation.**

The lies and insults are summarized this way: the history is inaccurate, Poles are depicted as pigs and collaborators with the Germans, and while the viciousness of the Holocaust was overwhelming, using this negative and biased way instructs children with a Polish ethnicity "that their people are morally debased and that their heritage is evil."

The Chairman, Board of Directors of The Catholic League is Walter Knysz Jr., and he is joined by Board of Directors members Alan Chesky and Richard Walawender, and Board of Advisor member Ronald Rychlak. All are Polish-American members of a great organization. Let us hope this will be the final attempt to get something destructive and harmful out of our schools and replace it with something better to teach that the Holocaust should "never again" happen.

Polish or Not?

If you read the Polish American Journal, you know there are exceptional Polish people of all stripes. Some even border on brilliant. When I heard about former Internal Revenue Service (IRS) Special Agent Chris Janczewski, that is how I felt.

Some of his major accomplishments with the IRS delt with uncovering scams to steal or launder billions of dollars in crypto currency held by individuals or companies but he was also instrumental in saving 25 children who were victims of child exploitation. This and other projects have not gone unnoticed by government officials.

Mr. Janczewski and his team's case work and methodologies were cited extensively in DOJ's "Cryptocurrency Enforcement Framework," and he has briefed policy makers at the highest levels of government on cryptocurrency and cyber issues. In recognition of his contributions, Mr. Janczewski has been the recipient of the The Secretary's Honor Award, from Secretary of the Treasury (2020), Chief's Investigative Excellence, from Chief, IRS - Criminal Investigation (2020), and the Meritorious Service Award, from Secretary of the Treasury (2019) among other awards.

Chris now works for TRM Labs (trmlabs.com) which is a digital asset compliance and risk management company. They "monitor, detect, and investigate crypto fraud and financial crime." Janczewski is the Head of Global Investigations. "One of the world's most accomplished cryptocurrency investigators," Chris Janczewski, Polish or not?

We have a few notable Polish inspired art pieces in the St. Louis area. One is the *The Angel of Harmony* by Wiktor Szostalo in the garden area next to the Cathedral Basilica of St. Louis and there is the Casimir Pulaski bust at the entrance to the Busey Bank (formerly Pulaski Bank) location in the city of

Creve Coeur in St. Louis County. Now we have *Hurrah!*, an interactive musical instrument installed on the grounds of Lindenwood University in St. Charles, Missouri, a western suburb of St. Louis.

Hurrah! is the work of Polish and American designers lead by Karol Murlak, professor at the Pratt Institute located in New York City, and was created to honor and observe one hundred years of diplomatic relations between the United States and Poland. Originally displayed in Times Square in New York City, it is a series of connected stainless steel tubes in differing heights and sizes, arranged in a circle, and as each tube is struck (as if playing a xylophone), the Polish birthday song *Sto Lat* is produced. One hundred years!

Per Professor Murlak, the "project is not about politics or even diplomacy. It is about being together and doing things together… Current events in Ukraine reminds us that Poland and the United States are still befriended and that it is good to have friends." I hope the sentiment and physical object last for more than one hundred years.

Can you sing me a Polish song, or not? Here is another use for the tune *Sto Lat*. Alice Kaminski, the matriarch of the Kaminski clan from St. Louis sent me a note about her granddaughter Julia who is a paramedic for one of the ambulance services in our city. Here is how Alice so eloquently described what happened to Julia while on duty.

She recently was on an emergency call to pick up and transport a patient who was in cardiac distress to a local hospital. Julia was stabilizing the patient in the ambulance when he noticed her name tag had a Polish last name. He asked her if she herself was Polish. She answered that she was. He asked her if she could sing him a Polish song. She answered that she could sing a song that her Diadziu and Babcia always sang with the family. In a soft and gentle voice, she started singing Sto Lat to him to comfort him.

According to Alice, with the song, the caring, and a "lovely" face, "it turns out there may be a sto lat for this patient." I know you did the Kaminski's proud with your work, but we are *all* proud of you Julia. God bless you and thank you for your service.

September 2022

Modern Polish church music.

My wife and I frequently attend the 11:30 Mass where they play mostly Christian rock. The priests at the parish, though, are of the stripe who are exceeding devout and will burst into a Latin chant at various parts of the liturgy. A strange mix you might think but it works: the music and worship are a beautiful spiritual experience. It is something different for me and I like it.

Over my lifetime the Catholic Church has been through at least three iterations of liturgical music. There were traditional songs from pre-Vatican II, in post Vatican II in the late sixties and seventies there was an effort to "modernize" the church with guitar-playing folksy tunes, and at one point and into the present we use the Jesuit hymnal with sprinkles of "Amazing Grace" and "How Great Thou Art" thrown in.

Knowing what great music the Poles have created, I was curious to know if there was anything happening in Poland, a very Catholic country, which would mimic creative periods we have experienced in the United States in the realm of liturgical music. A search on the web had one return for "modern Polish church music." The Extraordinary Music Workshop is a project initiated by the Dominican Liturgical Center in Krakow, Poland, "with the goal of creating new church music that brings back the stylistic traditions established by the Byzantine and Orthodox composers of yore." Their mission began in the 1990s and has produced over one thousand songs.

You can read more about it and hear snippets of some of the works produced at https://aleteia.org/2020/01/28/polish-dominicans-lead-a-campaign-for-new-liturgical-music. The project and the music are a combination of fellowship by using non-professional singers and musicians joined with prayerful and meditative choral compositions. It has also been described as "antiphonal," which is reminiscent of the short verses sung in the Latin Mass, for instance, which were used to bookend the beginning and end of the service. As various participants expressed their feelings,

The Polish Dominican style of writing is evocative not only in harmonies but in theology, meditation, and depth of text... they draw me into a prayerful and personal encounter with the Word of God... It is not afraid to claim our Catholic tradition, but also freely creates something new that corresponds to a world longing for its Redeemer.

The movement and workshops began in Poland but now is missionary-like in spreading the idea in America. There is an effort to expand to parishes and schools in the United States where the Dominicans serve. "This music is ideal for parishes to participate in experiencing the mysteries of our blessed Catholic faith with reverence and accessibility."

As excited as I am to hear about the "movement," I also need your help. The article referenced says that "audio files and scores will be available for listening, downloading, and free use in parishes around the English-speaking world." I cannot find any of it because the pandemic delayed it, or the production delayed for another reason. If you have access to where to get the English or Polish recordings and scores, please share. It is beautiful stuff and, biblically speaking, we must not hide it under a bushel basket.

Polish or Not?

If you are a regular fan of the hit show *America's Got Talent,* then you will know the name Sara James. Sara is from the small town of Osnie Lubuskie in Poland, has been taking piano lessons since she was six (go figure), and has already been in Polish and European voice competition shows. She auditioned for *America's Got Talent* at age 13 and was accepted for a spot in front of the judges.

Three fantastic things happen during her performance. After announcing that she was from Poland, both Simon Cowell and Howie Mandel said that they too had Polish ancestors. Then she wowed the audience with her rendition of the Billie Eilish song *Lovely* at which Simon reached over and smashed the golden buzzer. The Golden Buzzer is automatic acceptance to the live rounds and had been awarded only two other times during the 2022 season. It is quite a moment to witness, and it is available on YouTube if want to experience it. Lovely!

She is known as Huntergirl. Sounds like a character from the *The Hunger Games*, but no, she is a 2022 *American Idol* contestant whose real name is Hunter Wolkonowski. Hunter is the granddaughter of Chester Wolkonowski Jr., born in Rochester, New York. Chester Jr.'s parents are Chester Wolkonowski Sr., and Stella (Zalyski) Wolkonowski. I'm putting Hunter down for at least a Polish 25-percenter.

Hunter came in second, and while I hate second place, for that kind of competition and exposure, not too shabby. I predict, as bright as is her smile, so is her future. Go get 'em Huntergirl!!

In the Spring 2022 Abbey Banner magazine of the Saint John's monastic community located in Collegeville, Minnesota, is an article about the window on the north side of the Abbey and St. John's University Church. It is a famous church. The church was designed by the world-renowned architect, Marcel Breuer. However, the window, 468 hexagonal panels of stained glass (when built in 1962 it was the largest stained-glass window in North America), was the concept and design of a Polish born art professor at St. John's University, Bronislaw, "Bruno" Bak (Bonk).

Though the monks have been in Collegeville since 1857, the style of the window, like the church, has a very modern, Jackson Pollock look. Bak's impetus though came from something non-modern, the theme of worship:

... the title of this presentation: Sursum Corda or "Lift up Your Hearts," from the preface to the Eucharistic Prayer of the Mass. It is intended to be descriptive of the whole theme of the window – the theme of worship: the who, the why, the how, and the what of worship.

The ideas, the colors, and the glass arrangements, like the old and New Testament inspirations from which they come are broad and rich. It is all there, and it is beautiful. If you happen to be in central Minnesota any time soon, see the church and the Sursum Corda.

Surdyk's Liquors has been a fixture in the "Nordeast" of Minneapolis since 1934. While walking through the Minneapolis-St. Paul Airport I glanced over to see Surdyk's Wine Market & Bar. This expansion of the original store at the airport goes under the heading of Surdyk's Flights and has been a success. According to the Surdyk's Flights website https://surdyksflights.com/about,

Flights has won major awards including 1ˢᵗ place in the category of Best New Food and Beverage Concept by the Airports Council International in 2011, and The Airport Food & Beverage (FAB) Award for Best Airport Wine Bar in 2014.

Before your next connection, stop in Surdyk's Flights, have a Chardonnay, and take a load off. Surdyk's, Polish or not?

Another summer come and gone. Take it from me, they fly by the older you get. I am older. I will miss the fresh fruit and vegetables.

October 2022

Breaking and making bread.

By the way, in case you missed it, Sara James, *America's Got Talent* contestant and the girl from Poland, mentioned in last month's Pondering Pole, knocked 'em dead again with her rendition of Elton John's "Rocket Man." Trust me, it takes more to impress *me* than it does Simon Cowell and I was blown away. Whether she wins AGT or not, the youngster with the pretty face, the Polish accent, and the heavenly voice has made her mark.

There is a grocery store in St. Louis called Global Foods Market that specializes in "quality meats, dairy, produce, packaged goods, beer, wine, and candy" that is produced in countries from all over the planet. Their website does not say how many nations have flags hanging from the ceiling, but it must be around 30-40. Whenever I am there, it never fails to be a veritable collection of languages and looks that would rival a United Nations conclave.

Poland has goods on about a third of one of the aisles and there is a great selection of kielbasa in the deli. It is a place where I can get Polish rye (from the Racine Bakery in Chicago) and as always, in my latest trip to Global, I made a quick check of the bread section and spotted something called "Tarnowski." The label says it is made at Ideal Bakery, also in Chicago. It looked interesting so I bought a loaf.

Tarnowski ingredients include wheat & rye flour, salt, potatoes, water, and yeast. It is a slightly heavier, thicker bread because of the potatoes but had a wonderful crust and taste. I wanted to learn more about Tarnowski, why the name, and about the bakery. Visiting the website (https://www.idealbakery.net), made me pleasantly surprised. Ideal offers a whole bevy of breads with names like Grandma's Babuni Rye, Starogdanski, Lwowski, and Highlander/Zakopianski. The Zakopianski is described as an "Italian bread," but it is more Italian-like by virtue of the crust and soft texture. Zakopianski is Italian "inspired" though with Goral ingredients.

Also available is an "authentic" Polish rye, described as "Polish style rye makes you rethink everything you thought you knew about rye bread."

There is the Egg Twist Chalka, a raison bread, and Wiejski Rye, something akin to the basic bread making style and taste of the Poles from the villages and towns in rural Poland. The pictures of these varieties of bread look deliciously like the shots of those you see at artisan bakeries.

Then, like Alice in Wonderland, viewing and discovering the breads at Ideal made me curiouser and curiouser (or ponderinger and ponderinger), and I searched "Polish bread" on the web. Among others, there were a couple very interesting returns. One was entitled *12 Traditional Polish Breads* on the Insanely Good website (https://insanelygoodrecipes.com/polish-breads). The article starts out by saying, "Whether you realize it or not, Polish breads are a huge deal." This site gives a tantalizing display and description of the twelve breads, mostly familiar but has a recipe available as well for making them.

Another one that I found excellent was called *6 Most Popular Polish Breads* from the Taste Atlas website (https://www.tasteatlas.com/most-popular-breads-in-poland). *6 Most* similarly shows a beautiful picture of the bread and a description, but it also includes information on what is the region or place of origin. These are exotic looking loafs or rolls with names such as Chleb Pradnicki, Zymla, Podplomyk, Proziaki, and Cebularz Lubelski, "a round-shaped flatbread with a thickness of about 1.5 centimeters. It is produced in the Lublin Province in Poland, and only 24 bakeries make this unique product that should be eaten fresh, as it must be consumed within 48 hours of being baked."

Probably the simplest of the six bread versions but one that obliges me to find or make it is the Obwarzanek Krakowski, or the Polish bagel. Hey, according to Taste Atlas, it is not just like any "regular" bagel. "It is bigger than the standard bagels and is woven from two strands of dough instead of just one. Before being baked, it is boiled and can be additionally sprinkled with poppy or sesame seeds, herbs, spices, cheese, salt, or onions. It has a sweetish taste and a dense, chewy texture." Cream cheese anyone?

Happy Polish Heritage Month!! Dziekuje bardzo to Chris at Ideal Bakery for the enlightening conversation about owning a Polish bakery in Chicago. Here's an idea. Jump on one of the web sites mentioned above and bake some bread for Polish Heritage Month. If you are not that ambitious and you are from Chicago, stop by the Racine or Ideal Bakery and buy a loaf or two. You won't be disappointed. If you are versed in baking Polish breads and can add to what was presented today, please share. Remember, Polish breads are a BIG DEAL and so is our Polish heritage!

November 2022

Legendary hurricanes and their trackers.

Not sure how I missed it, but the Dominican Liturgical Center Foundation website gives you the opportunity to download some of the music and scores that are part of the Extraordinary Music Workshop project. This link, https://dlc.foundation/product/soul-of-christ, will enable you to listen to the album *Soul of Christ* on Spotify and download the sheet music to the songs. "We know that this music will transform the prayer life of singers and congregation alike through its powerful, meditative beauty." May you be transformed, and it is free.

Why, since I became a seasoned citizen and retired from my regular job so I could take on more work, I find myself monitoring the weather more regularly and with greater scrutiny. Hurricane Ian was the latest in super immense and destructive storms to strike the American mainland, this time on the west side of Florida, in and around Fort Meyers. It was over the many days of reporting that I caught the back end of an interview with an extreme weather event expert named Jeff Piotrowski. There are legions of weather reporters, forecasters, and meteorologists, but Jeff Piotrowski a legend among them as a tornado and hurricane tracker.

This important part of his life where he "started shooting extreme weather began on June 8, 1974" when he was fourteen years old. Since then, from the Twister Chasers website (https://www.twisterchasers.com/jeff-piotrowski.html), he has amassed the –

> *largest private collection of historic weather events and survivors' stories. In 1994 Jeff received an Emmy award for "Day of Tornadoes" for his coverage of the Gainesville TX F2 tornado. More than likely, you have watched Jeff's footage in numerous productions on The Discovery Channel, National Geographic notably National Geographic Special "Witness: The Joplin Tornado", The History Channel, TLC as well as all major news networks, Insurance Ads and PSAs.*

During a severe weather event Jeff is a "regular guest" on Wolf Blitzer, Anderson Cooper, and Piers Morgan.

In addition, over the last 45 years, he has filmed over 1,000 tornados and 62 landfalling hurricanes. Born in Tulsa, Oklahoma, the grandson of Polish immigrants on his father's side, he started out as a home contractor, was a land developer, and sells "weather radar systems, displays, and digital APP data across North America." He currently works for Baron Weather in Huntsville, Alabama.

We are fascinated by what people like Jeff Piotrowski do (Steven Spielberg made a movie about it) but it is harrowing and dangerous and, in the end, besides the thrill of it and the notoriety, his understanding, experience, and reporting about extreme weather saves lives. That makes it all worth it.

Polish or Not?

Another big event in the last month, and involves weather, was the death of Elizabeth II, Queen of England. Her majesty's life was the perfect combination of fairy tale and epic tale. That was the public view of her doing the "job," but we were also privy throughout her reign to slices of her every-day life and personality. One of the funny and delightful stories to come out during the twilight of her life was her keen interest in viewing the Polish-British TV meteorologist Tomasz Schafermaker. It was rumored that Elizabeth had a "bit of a crush" on the weatherman. Replied Tomasz to the affections by the Queen, "truly heartwarming."

V
2023

January 2023

The love of all things that are...

For you love all things that are and loathe nothing that you have made; for what you hated, you would not have fashioned. And how could a thing remain, unless you willed it; or be preserved, had it not been called forth by you?

Book of Wisdom 11:22-12:2

The homily at Mass today was excellent and centered on these lines from the first reading, the Book of Wisdom. Normally when we talk about believers in God, we think in terms of receiving, acknowledging, or accepting, as in God the Father, of the Old Testament, or as in the New Testament, of Christ as Redeemer and Savior, and thus becoming a Christian. Soon we will celebrate the birth of Jesus; God sent down to earth to dwell among us. We receive Him. Faith, in all these cases is a reaction to things learned or felt by the believer.

The verses though, speak of how we already belong to God and have always been in the mind and heart of God. We have always been there, wrinkles and all, sinners, and saints, the love of all things that are. That does not diminish what is required by us to become active or practicing people of faith, or even good people, but it does add a perspective and another side of the equation, a refreshing side, a reassuring side.

By comparison, we tend to take on the trappings of our ethnicity and culture by our names, language, history, or customs. In that way we receive our Polishness. Sometimes we gladly accept it, sometimes we reluctantly acknowledge it, and sometimes we dismiss it.

On the other side of this equation though, there can be no denying that to be Polish is already within us, that we already belong. It is preordained and present and if we really want to match the beauty and essence in what is in scripture, then we know that it was willed, fashioned, and preserved by God. No matter what any detractor or denier might say, there is a place called Poland, and a people, and it is a creation "made" and blessed by the love of God. Isn't *that* a refreshing idea and one to meditate on this Christmas.

In September and October of this year we observed the efforts of Sara James, 16-year-old singer from Poland, and contestant on the television show, *America's Got Talent*. Sara did not make the final five, but she certainly made her mark with the judges and fans. Besides her renditions of *Lovely* and *Rocket Man*, available on YouTube, I would also suggest you listen to her other songs, those done all or mostly in Polish. You will be pleasantly surprised, and it is confirmation that she is the real deal, whatever the language, whatever the country. Sara is amazing, and another amazing Polish singer, is a young man who goes only by the name, Ochman.

His full name is Krystian Jan Ochman, and although he is extremely popular in Poland, and both of his parents are Polish, surprisingly he was born in Melrose, Massachusetts, in the United States. Like Sara James, he used *The Voice of Poland* and the *Eurovision Song Contest* competitions as a springboard for better things, which in his case resulted in a contract with Universal Music Polska, a subsidiary of Universal Music Group, one of the three largest music corporations in the world along with Sony Music and Warner Music Group.

As you listen to his songs you will quickly realize he has a strong, clear, but full-ranging voice and the best evidence of this is in the song co-written by him, "River." There is considerable talk by the YouTubers that this will be a hit not only in Poland, but in Europe, and beyond. It is important to point out, Ochman is the grandson of Wieslaw Ochman, a famous Polish tenor of the national and international stage, who performed at the Opera Krakowska, the Paris Opera, *La Scala* in Milan, Italy, and the Metropolitan Opera in New York City. Krystian Ochman has the looks, the pipes, and the pedigree to make it big. We will be waiting, by the river or wherever, for his next big thing.

Polish or Not?

Last year I wrote about a couple of cartoon characters in computer-animated films that had Polish surnames, to wit, Mike Wazowski of *Monsters University*, and the Pudowski family in *Ron's Gone Wrong*. Both excellent flicks and positive Polish props. Did not see *The Lego Movie* and only saw bits and pieces of *The Lego Movie 2: The Second Part*. The 2014 and 2019 films were produced by Warner Bros. Pictures, and the main lead in both is Emmett Brickowski, described as a "friendly, jolly, innocent, sweet, and optimistic individual; initially an ordinary, everyman citizen just trying to do his job… He is kind to everyone for most of the time, even towards his enemies, and never seems to hold a grudge."

All these traits along with he is a master builder, smart, determined, and feels that "*everything* is awesome." Of course, his name is Brickowski! Go Emmett and good luck with all you have going in Lego world.

Roblox is an online game creation, game sharing, and social interaction program co-created by David Baszucki in 2004. *Roblox*, owned by Roblox Corporation has become a huge player in the computer video gaming industry.

It is different from other gaming software that users, mostly youngsters, and teenagers, can create games themselves and then share them with others. The idea has been lauded by some as a positive "contribution to education, and encouraging kids to code," thus empowering children and teenagers, but has been criticized for "exploiting child game developers," among others.

Baszucki was born January 20, 1963, in Canada but spent his early childhood and teenage years in Eden Prairie, Minnesota. He is CEO of Roblox Corporation which holds fifteen patents and has a market valuation of twenty-two billion. He has received numerous awards, is an avid mountain biker, and is worth somewhere between four hundred million and 9 billion dollars. David Baszucki, Polish or not?

A belated Wesoly Swiat to you and your family and I hope you feel the love of God, especially during the holidays, not because you have become something, or need to do something, but only because you are part of the love of "all things that are."

February 2023

"And the winner is... "

The Turner Classic Movies (TCM) channel is one of my favorites. The "classics" are part of every era and time-period but what makes them so great varies by who is determining it and by what criteria. There is a documentary film on TCM entitled *Women Make Film: A New Road Movie Through Cinema* with the sub-title "A guided tour of the art of movie creation as told by female filmmakers" that "explores 40 different aspects of filmmaking, drawing from a wide range of films as examples, all which are made by women." Some of the movies can be considered classic as a whole and some have one or several classic elements that are remarkable.

The documentary was created by filmmaker and critic Mark Cousins and features the contributions and innovations of 183 directors from all over the world since movie making began. That there are 183 women directors recognized in the documentary is a revelation to me. Not the work but the sheer number! Impressive. What I saw on TCM was a one-hour summary of the original which is 14 hours long. The film is divided into "chapters," or as mentioned, "aspects" of filmmaking such as Introduction, Openings, Tone, Believability, and Conversation.

Many of the director names are familiar: Kathryn Bigelow, Jane Campion, Sofia Coppola, Leni Riefenstahl, Angelina Jolie, and Penny Marshall. Had no idea that Ida Lupino was a director and no idea that, despite the name, her ethnicity is British and Irish. Surprisingly, two greats of world cinema, Agnieszka Holland of Poland and Lina Wertmuller of Italy were not featured. Four Polish gals were, however, and here are their names, the films which were special to this project, and for what category or aspect that made their work notable.

Dorota Kedzierzawska, *Time to Die*, (2007; Openings, Memory, Death). Pani Kedzierzawska was born June 1, 1957, in Lodz and graduated from the prestigious National Film School in Lodz. *Time to Die* is a "black-and-white portrait of the day-to-day of a nonagenarian woman as she experiences the final act of her life," especially in her interactions with neighbors, her son, and her dog, Fila.

Wanda Jakubowska, *The Last Stage*, (1948; Openings, Framing, Bodies). Jakubowska was born November 10, 1907, and died February 1998. She directed 15 films over her career and was the first female director to be nominated for an Academy Award in 1933 for her short film *The Sea*. A member of the Polish underground army during World War II, she was captured, imprisoned, and spent time as an inmate at Auschwitz and Ravensbruck. Her work, *The Last Stage* "was an early and influential depiction of concentration camps."

Malgorzata Szumowska, *Body*, (2015; Comedy). A native of Krakow, she was born February 26, 1973. Like Kiedzierzawska, she is an alum of the National Film School in Lodz. Szumowska has won numerous awards for her films and won the Berlin International Film Festival *Silver Bear for Best Director* award for *Body*. It is a story about a woman, the daughter of an attorney, with a psychiatric condition who is treated by a therapist who is dealing with issues herself and thinks she can communicate with ghosts. Perhaps funny but wacky for sure.

Hanna Polak, *Something Better to Come*, (2014; Time). Written, produced, and directed by Polak, *Something* is a documentary film about children who live in a Moscow garbage dump. The story follows the struggles and challenges of the main character Yula for 14 years as her life is juxtaposed with the rule of Vladimir Putin. Hanna Polak has been nominated for an Academy Award and an Emmy Award and has received several other awards for her documentary films. She was born in Katowice in 1967.

You can learn more about these fine directors, Kiedzierzawska, Jakubowska, Szumowska, and Polak, and the films acknowledged in the *Women Make Film* documentary in Wikipedia, the IMDB website, and they are featured online at Culture.pl. Besides these four movies, each has a body of work and a story you might want to experience and enjoy. They are a credit to Polonia, a credit to their craft as are all the 183 female directors, but more so, for those of us that appreciate the power and magic of the movies.

Polish or Not?

As this is written, NCAA college football is winding down and the Michigan Wolverines are 13-1, led by coach Jim Harbaugh. Besides being an outstanding college player, Harbaugh was also a National Football League quarterback and, if true, joins the 25-percenter Polish "quarterback" club along with Tom Brady and Tony Romo who also have one parent with half Polish ancestry. According to Wikipedia, Jim's mom is half-Sicilian and half-Polish.

Probably going to get into a lot of trouble for doing this but GO WOLVERINES!

Also presented on Turner Classic Movies was a series of films by the great Italian director Federico Fellini. The showing of Fellini's *Juliet of the Spirits* is an interesting movie and a joy to watch and was part of his "dreams" period. One thing that caught my attention was the name of Sylva Koscina during the paging of the introductory cast.

According to Wikipedia, Sylva was born in Yugoslavia, August 22, 1933, but to a Greek father and a Polish mother. She moved to Italy during World War II to live with her sister who was married to an Italian national. In Italy she won beauty contests, did modeling work, studied physics at the University of Naples, and began her acting career in 1954 after being noticed by director Eduardo De Filippo.

The beautiful, intelligent, and talented Koscina appeared in over one hundred films in and outside of Italy with her final performance in *Kim Novak Is on the Phone* in 1994. Fantastico!

Ah, the Rat Pack. Super attractive, entertaining, likable, lovable guys, tough guys like Sinatra, Martin, Davis, Lawford, and… Joey Bishop. Born Joseph Abraham Gottlieb, February 3, 1918, and according to Wikipedia, he was "the son of Polish-Jewish immigrants Anna (nee Siegel) and Jacob Gottlieb."

Bishop was among the stars of the original Ocean's 11… During filming, the five entertainers performed together onstage in Vegas at the Sands Hotel. Bishop did only a little singing and dancing, but he told jokes and wrote most of the act's material.

I think of Joey Bishop as the other guy in the Rat Pack and maybe that is because he is one of our guys.

I saw Steve Kornacki on one of the sports channels giving his "line" on which NFL teams would make the playoffs. He did some nifty calculations on what each team's percentages were for the balance of the season. A gregarious personality, Stephan Joseph Kornacki is a journalist, writer, and television presenter, born in Groton, Massachusetts. According to the website Married Bio (https://marriedbio.com/steve-kornacki-biography), Steve Kornacki is Polish.

May you have a loving and sweet Valentine's Day by telling your favorite female (wife, mother, sister, friend, film director), ja cie kocham.

March 2023

Changing the historical narrative.

*I*t wasn't that long ago I had a "debate" with one of my *Polish* friends on whether the Poles charged the German tanks with their cavalry at the start of World War II. He insisted this was correct because he saw it on – television. I don't think I convinced him otherwise that what he learned and therefore believed might not be true.

Can't blame him really. How he came to that conclusion is indicative in many cases on how we learn. Life should be a search for the truth, encompassing all methods, and open to every point of view; for many it is sadly derived and accepted only from information on the TV, the internet, what so-and-so said, or conviction by "feeling." All I can do for him now is give him the book, *Poland 1939*, by Roger Moorhouse (Basic Books, New York, 2020).

There are numerous great histories about the Poles in World War II but this one is different because it was specific to the "war" of Germany and Russia, against Poland in 1939. I have read many books about the American Civil War and in most of them concerning battles and generals there is detail about the positions and movements of the combatants including analysis and commentary to explain the military engagements. This is how *Poland 1939* is organized.

Suffice it to say the Poles were overwhelmed by the Germans and Russians. On the positive side though, Poland's armies usually were able to hold or beat back their adversaries in battles at least initially. Then, when ammunition and supplies ran low, they were pushed back to a defensive position or defeated. There were examples of incredible bravery and determination. Polish cavalry units were effective in certain circumstances and battles. This was the pattern throughout.

For the negative, the Poles fought based on World War I strategy, communication among army groups was poor or non-existent, German superiority of the air was far more important and devastating than the fabled armored blitzkrieg, and the quality and quantity of equipment and supplies was greatly lacking not allowing them to sustain any gains or establish viable fronts. There is much, much more to this story and you can read about it. Here are a few of my personal highlights from the book that perhaps you can use in your own "debates."

Allies – The support of the British and French towards their ally Poland after Germany invaded was inept or non-existent. According to Moorhouse, Hitler threw the bulk of his army at the Polish campaign and the western part of Germany was scantily defended. If the French attacked and the British bombed, perhaps the whole story of the second World War would have been much different. All accusations that the Poles did not "do enough" during the entire World War II and the Holocaust are trumped by this simple fact.

The destruction of Warsaw – We think of the destruction of Warsaw during the uprising of August 1, 1944, but the true story, as General Sosabowski remarked, by the end of September, 1939, "everything was destroyed or damaged, dead or dying." That was also true of most of the country as the Germans bombed and burned cities and villages indiscriminately whether militarily significant or not. Warsaw, "The Paris of the East," was "no longer recognizable."

Prisoners of war – A minority of Polish soldiers were lucky and sent home after capture. Many others "would ultimately find themselves dragooned as slave laborers and deported to Hitler's Germany, where they would endure a punishing existence on farms and in factories in conditions that often mimicked those in the concentration camps." The murder of the Polish officers at the hands of the Russians at Katyn was horrible, but where are the monuments to the enlisted men and officers who were exterminated at the hands of the Einsatzgruppen?

Cavalry – As mentioned, the Polish cavalry was generally useful and effective during the war, and no, it did not charge tanks. Here though, is a bit of trivia that is tantalizing pertaining to this subject: At the battle of Tomaszow-Lubelski, "At dawn on a foggy morning, a two-pronged cavalry charge at German positions on the outskirts of the town soon had the enemy in retreat, pursued by saber-wielding Uhlans. The Polish advance was temporarily checked by a countercharge by elements of the German 17th cavalry regiment, making it one of the last cavalry-on-cavalry engagements in history." In case you are wondering, no, the Germans did not attack Polish tanks with their cavalry.

Enigma – Moorhouse states, "Polish mathematicians – Henryk Zygalski, Jerzy Rozycki, and Marian Rejewski – who had been working to crack the German Enigma encryption machine for the Cypher Bureau of the Polish General Staff… vital work that Rejewski, Zygalski, and Rozycki did on the German Enigma codes would, according to some estimates, shortened the war by perhaps two years." Not sure who made those estimates, but if credible, is as huge a contribution in saving lives and property as any of the other monumental events of the war: The Battle for Britain, Stalingrad, D-Day, Midway, or Hiroshima.

Perhaps the last and best question was posed by a Warsaw housewife, "If we haven't got the right arms, why did we dare to stand up to them?" No one knows what the outcome of any war will be. The Poles undoubtedly knew the strength and capacity of the German military complex leading up to 1939. Culture and tradition, the victory over the Russians in 1920, and the reports and the hope for reports of the participation of their allies led them to fight and unfortunately in some cases to keep fighting.

If you are Polish, Roger Moorhouse has provided an excellent source of information on what happened in Poland leading up to and during the beginning of World War II. Militarily, what transpired after was not that much different in the other European countries facing one of the greatest armies of all time. As I finished reading the book though, I couldn't stop thinking of other conflicts and especially the current war in Ukraine. "If we haven't got the right arms, why did we dare to stand up to them?" Does history repeat itself?

DNA Diary.

As they say on the cable news network – Breaking News! and when determination pays off. Terrance "Terry" Pegula, billionaire owner of the Buffalo Bills NFL team, the NHL Buffalo Sabres hockey team, and father of pro-tennis star Jessica Pegula has a Polish mom. Crack researcher Jack Jackowski found this information.

> *Terry Pegula's mother's maiden name is Eloise De Cavage. Her father is Joseph De Cavage. According to the 1910 census: Polish was spoken in the home & her father's birthplace was Russia - Poland. Her mother, Anna Shinoski, was born in Austria - Poland. She is*

buried in a Pennsylvania Polish cemetery. To be clear, Terry Pegula's mother had a Polish mother & father.

Terry Pegula was born in Carbondale, Pennsylvania, and began his career as a petroleum engineer. His other "interests" are in natural gas development, real estate, and entertainment.

Can't tell you how many times I have gone through the Catholic hymnal *Glory and Praise* looking for a Polish named songwriter. While this music book has a wide variety of traditional works and composers, it is popularly known for the modern sound, reference to scriptural verse, and full of catchy tunes especially by a group called the St. Louis Jesuits, John Foley, Dan Schutte, Roc O'Connor, Tim Mannion, and Bob Dufford. Not part of that group, but a Jesuit, catchy tune writer as well, and apparently Polish, is Michael Joncas. According to Wikipedia,

Joncas was raised in Minneapolis, of Polish descent, attending Nazareth Hall Preparatory Seminary and St. John Vianney Seminary at the University of St. Thomas, earning a bachelor's degree in English there in 1975.

He is best known for the most beautiful melody and words, "On Eagles Wings," which I believe is sung every other Sunday during the Liturgical year. My other Joncas favorite, also in *Glory and Praise*, is "I Have Loved You." God bless the Jesuits and especially those from Minnesota.

Another Polish rocker. This is so-o-o cool. What must it feel like to be part of a group that boasts such greats as Jeff Beck, Eric Clapton, and Jimmy Page. The other guys weren't slouches either, Keith Relf, Jim McCarty, Paul Samwell-Smith, and… Chris Dreja. All proper English gentlemen and original or former members of The Yardbirds, a "rock band, formed in London in 1963." Dreja, however, was only half an English gentleman.

His father, Alojzy Dreja (1918–1985), was from Poland; he had been exiled to Britain in 1940, and served as a pilot in the Polish Air Force in Great Britain during World War II. Chris Dreja's brother Stefan happened to meet guitarist Top Topham when they studied at the same pre-college art program, and introduced him to his brother. Topham and Dreja were influenced by folk/blues

> *guitarist Gerry Lockran, who influenced them to switch from acoustic to electric guitars... Dreja and Topham became core members of the Metropolitan (or Metropolis) Blues Quartet. During the space of a year Keith Relf, Jim McCarty, and Paul Samwell-Smith joined the group which became the Yardbirds. The 15-year-old Topham left the group when the band went professional, but Dreja continued on to play rhythm guitar with musicians such as Eric Clapton and later Jeff Beck and Jimmy Page.*

Dreja was inducted into the Rock and Roll Hall of Fame in 1992. After The Yardbirds, he pursued a career in photography and, for the record, he turned down an offer from Jimmy Page to play bass in a silly little band that would later become - Led Zeppelin.

April 2023

And He will raise you up.

The title is a line from the song "On Eagle's Wings" and the perfect sentiment to think about at Easter.

Last month I told you about the composer for the great religious songs "On Eagle's Wings," and "I Have Loved You," the Catholic American priest, (Jan) Michael Joncas. Father Michael graciously eMailed me with more information regarding his life and music.

First, he is a retired priest from the archdiocese of St. Paul-Minneapolis with a "40-year ministry teaching theology and Catholic studies at the University of St. Thomas in St. Paul." He also taught at St. John's University in Collegeville, Minnesota, my alma mater. He is not a Society of Jesus order priest (Jesuit) as I thought, that mistake probably because he is in the *Glory and Praise* hymnal, and because he is a teacher. The Jesuits are a teaching order.

Besides his tenure as a professor, he has degrees from the College of St. Thomas, University of Notre Dame, and the Pontifico Instituto Liturgico of the Ateneo St. Anselmo in Rome. Father Joncas has written six books, over two hundred fifty articles, and has "composed and arranged more than 300 pieces of liturgical music."

Regarding his ethnicity, I suppose I passed him over so many times thinking he could not be Polish because of the name Joncas. No matter how hard I tried, I could not make it "fit" for a Polish name as it is spelled, or a part of a Polish name, or a revised Polish name. "I'm descended from a Basque named Pierre Joncas... " and so Michael Joncas, with other French connections, is French on his father's side.

Mother's mom and dad, Josef and Rosalia Narog, were immigrants from Poland. While Dziadzia Josef died early in his life, his association with Grandma produced rich memories of phrases and prayers in Polish. Speaking of Polish names, "Notice that my legal name is Jan Michael, the first name obviously being the Polish form of "John." So where did the propensity for writing music come from?

I ascribe my love of music to my mother, a lyric soprano who pretty much gave up her career to raise us 8 kids. I have wonderful memories of her singing around the house and in church, including Kolendy at Christmastime.

In case you are wondering, "On Eagle's Wings" was written for the funeral of a close friend's father and "I Have Loved You" was on behalf of the "Franciscan Sisters of Rochester, MN, as a 'theme song' for their 'chapter of mats' (community meeting)… " "Blessings" and a heartfelt dziekuje bardzo Father Jan Michael Joncas for contributing so much to the service and worship of the Catholic Christian community.

DNA Diary.

I snag a copy of *Feast Magazine* (feastmagazine.com, published in St. Louis, Missouri) whenever available and in the January 2023, issue was a piece about Twarog, "Polish-style farmer's cheese made from cow's milk." It most closely resembles Italian ricotta, quark (low-fat soft cheese), and cottage cheese, "although the flavour is quite unique and it's hard to compare it to any other cheese" as it is a "creation not found anywhere else in the world." It is typically used in pierogi, cheesecake, nalesniki, breads, and spreads. *Feast* featured recipes for "Goose Feet Farmer's Cookies" and "Herbed Pancake Bites with Eggs and Salmon."

If you want to try out Twarog in your next cooking project, the web has ample information on this subject but to get you started here are several sites to visit: *The Polish Housewife* (https://polishhousewife.com/twarog-polish-farmers-cheese/), *The Polonist* (https://www.polonist.com/farmers-cheese-twarog), and *Tasteatlas* (https://www.tasteatlas.com/twarog). You should find instructions on how to make your own Twarog and you will probably find other delectable ingredients and recipes to please your Polish palate and tummy. Smacznego!!

I'm looking at a Menard's ad and at the back of their flyer is the grocery items. "Polish" sauerkraut is on sale and that reminded me about spotting Frank's "Polish" sauerkraut on the shelf at Walmart. You can get Polish style sauerkraut at the international stores in the Poland aisle of course but to see it produced by the American manufacturers is, I think, a big deal. Another Polish mainstream item for sale in the United States economy.

It wasn't that long ago that I wrote about the difference between Kosher and Polish pickles. The difference is minor you might recall. We think of sauerkraut as being German so what is the difference between German and Polish style kraut? What we usually buy in the grocery store is a simple variation of both but heavy on vinegar and other preservatives. Traditional sauerkraut is pickled cabbage with the key ingredient, brine.

I found it hard to find precise definitions for what constitutes a German version or a Polish version but the closest I came to distinguishing the two is that German has carraway seeds and juniper berries added and Polish kraut is made with shredded cabbage and carrots but can also have beets added, the "red" sauerkraut. There are many and varied recipes but here is my cousin Jody's Polish grandma's recipe (on her mom's side) for kraut which I thoroughly enjoy when she serves it. This is the "crowd" amount.

> *4 cans of kraut. 4-5 meaty neck bones. Brown the neck bones in a tad of butter in your stock pot. Take neck bones out and sauté about 3 medium onions or 2 large YELLOW onions (if you use Vidalia sweet onions it makes it too sweet.) and a couple cloves of garlic. Depending on how sour you want your kraut you rinse the kraut before adding to the stock pot. I usually rinse two and leave two. I do drain them though. Add chicken broth or stock and the neck bones to the pot before adding your kraut. You want enough stock to cover as you are going to let this simmer or cook for a while. I usually leave it on the stove for a couple of hours. I also add a large potato or a couple of small ones diced very small. The potato will help thicken the kraut. I also throw in some dried parsley flakes. I just add pepper as the chicken broth or stock usually has enough salt for me. You can tell when the kraut is done. It usually gets a little darker. When your neck bones are finished cooking and the kraut is ready take out the neck bones. I usually pull whatever meat off the bones I can and leave that in the kraut. ENJOY!*

Hope you enjoy as well. A nice reference on the subject of kraut is on the website called *An Affair from the Heart*, (https://anaffairfromtheheart.com/the-ultimate-guide-to-sauerkraut) owned by Michaela Kenkel who happens to be half German and half Polish. How perfect is that! She is amazing in so many ways and you can find other great recipes on this site.

Best Of…

VI

2013

January 2013

Milestones.

Dzien Dobry 2013. I woke up the other day and realized that I had worked for the same company for 25 years! Where did the time go? It feels like 24.

A red-letter day like that instills a wonderful sense of calm, satisfaction, and accomplishment. It wasn't always easy, and I certainly wish I had done more than a few things differently in those twenty-five years but on balance, it feels good and was a pretty good ride. I said it felt like 24 and a smiley face truly would be apropos because it felt more like five years. Where *did* the time go?

Nestled in with the calm, the satisfaction, and the accomplishment though, is a sudden sense of urgency as well. The urgency comes from the fact that there is a lot more to accomplish and the realization that time is running out. The longer you are in the game and experience so many things in life, the greater the possibilities seem and greater are the expectations. This is the other side of the coin.

Our Polonia is the same way. Looking back as the "grandchild" of the immigrants, experiencing the culture, learning the culture, involved in the culture, yes, there is a sense of calm and satisfaction now, but I also feel the necessity to "complete" the one hundred year immigration experience that Michael Novak talks about in the *Unmeltable Ethnics* (Pondering Pole, October 2012). If you figure that most of our people came here around 1925 and we are quickly approaching the 2025-mark, time is running out. Dziadzia and grandma ain't around anymore and the moms, dads, uncles, and aunts are fading away now as well. No one is going to help us on the last lap, whatever that might be.

So where are we headed? What is left to complete? I believe we have made a mark as individuals and as a community and have established our legacy in contributing to the greatness of this country. It is not hard to mention one or more outstanding Poles in almost any discipline or area of interest. I guess that final milestone I would want to reach is a total and unqualified acceptance of our ethnicity and what we bring culturally to society. That would be the capper.

Rather than us just dissolve into the American scene, I want us to be an identifiable piece in the fabric of the society. I'd like us to get to a point of no more changing the names to "help our careers"; no more belittling ourselves to pre-empt or diffuse poor behavior; yes more success incorporating Polish things and characteristics; and as easy as it flows off the tongue for someone talking about being Irish or Jewish, yes to being relaxed and uninhibited speaking about the Polish.

We are on our way, and I am encouraged. The light is getting brighter and brighter at the end of the tunnel and here are a few examples of the kinds of things that make me feel good about the future:

SelectQuote Life insurance company (http://selectquote.com) has a radio commercial featuring a representative "Nick Soloweski" (sp?) finding a great deal for a customer. Ford Motor Company runs a television commercial featuring innovations by employee "Scott Makowski." Polish names selling products.

Ren Behan's FABULICIOUS FOOD! (http://www.renbehan.com/) is a blog featuring modern and creative Polish cooking. The web site offers upscale versions of "Seasonally inspired home cooking, recipes, reviews & food writing." What I like most is the look of the web site and the shots of the various dishes are done exquisitely as if right out of "Bon Appetit" only with Polish filling. Check it out!

Bernie Miklasz, ESPN show host and writer for the St. Louis Post-Dispatch claimed the number one spot (over second place, none other than, Bob Costas!) in the October 18, 2012 issue of the St. Louis Riverfront Times "2012 RFT St. Louis Sports Media Power Rankings" (http://www.riverfronttimes.com/microsites/power_rankings/). "Be it radio, TV or print, the 'Big Dog' holds fan base and franchises alike in his sway." Yet this prevalent Pole keeps his toe in the ethnic waters as an Honorary Chairperson for the Polish Heritage Golf Tournament each year.

If you are looking for projects and tasks for the coming year and beyond, eMail me. Be advised, the pay is terrible but the emotional and psychological benefits are great.

Polish or Not?

Meg Ryan, actress (When Harry Met Sally, Sleepless in Seattle), is she Polish or not? Well, she is Polish according to Ethnic Celebs (http://ethnicelebs.com). "She was born Margaret Mary Emily Hyra, and took on Anne as a confirmation name. Meg's paternal grandparents were Michael Orest Hyra (the son of Orest Hyra and Anna "Annie" Durniak) and Mary Helen. Orest Hyra was born in Galicia, Halychyna, Poland, the son of Georgi Hyra and Katarzyna Fylak. Annie Durniak was also likely of Polish descent." The Ryan part comes from Meg's mom whose maiden name was Ryan. At best, Meg is Irish and Polish, but EC does not specify whether mom was 100% Irish.

March 2013

Farewell to the "Perfect Knight."

Stan Musial, Stan "The Man," died, January 19, 2013. May he rest in peace.

Please indulge me with some thoughts on the passing of baseball's "Perfect Knight," a real hometown hero, "The Man," ninety-two years young. Even as a St. Louisan and Cardinal fan I was amazed at the outpouring of adulation and respect the city and the media paid him in our town. Many of the Cardinal greats including his good friend Red Schoendienst, Whitey Herzog, Ozzie Smith, Joe Torre, and Tony LaRussa, spoke about him as a great guy, a fun guy, a perfect role model, a giving man, and mostly just a good and decent person.

Bob Costas did a truly heartfelt eulogy at the Mass. Julian Javier, Cardinal second baseman in the 50s and 60s, named his son after Stan. Musial was the favorite player and influence for the Pittsburgh Pirate's great first baseman, Willie Stargell. The St. Louis Blues hockey team all wore number 6 jerseys during their warmup for the game on the Saturday night following the funeral Mass. A reporter asked Stan's grandson if he liked hockey and he said he did but didn't like to go to the games because of the fighting. Of course, and that made perfect sense for a Musial.

Everyone had a story about Stan. It seems like they were never ending. Bob Costas, in a radio interview, told of Musial's admiration for of all people, Mickey Mantle. He spoke about how Stan felt a connection with the way they grew up, their father's hard lives, and how Mantle impressed him as a ball player. Costas did the eulogy at Mantle's funeral, and about halfway through, while struggling to keep his composure at the loss of *his* idol, he panned the congregation and fixed on Musial, sitting in a chair in the left aisle of the church, by himself, present, solemn, paying his respects. He flew in on the day of the funeral and then quietly left shortly afterward to go home. Mantle and Musial were only acquaintances and were certainly different animals in their personal lives, but he came because he thought a lot of his idol, Mickey Mantle.

On and on, the accolades, the way he affected others, the stories, and though usually just a mention, there is Stan, the "Polish" man. St. Louis Polonia will always remember Stan for what he did for us. He made appearances at St. Stanislaus Kostka Church, at the Polish American Cultural Society Polonez Ball, and at the Polish Heritage Open (PHO) Golf Tournament. He was the honorary chairman of the PHO for many years and helped with various donations of his memorabilia for our auction. I believe his ethnic background was something he felt as well as acknowledged. Son of an immigrant Pole, Musial did not forget where he came from, whether from St. Louis, Donora Pennsylvania, or Poland.

Barrett Jackman of the Blues said, "Stan was thought of as a god around here" and though there was a certain amount of truth to that he wasn't a god, and we all have to go some time. We will miss him and cherish the many times that he took us "out to the ballgame." Goodbye friend and thank you for giving so much of yourself to so many for so long.

April 2013

Linkage.

The passing and tribute to Stan Musial in January prompted a Pondering Pole question, not appropriate then, but appropriate now. If Stan was so popular, admired, and respected, why isn't Poland? It should follow that if you thought so highly of someone, and that person comes from a place, wouldn't you think the place had to be special?

Not by everyone of course but you must admit, most Americans when the words Poland or Polish are spoken don't get the kind of reaction and respect that, let's say, Italy, Mexico, Ireland, England, Russia, or Israel get when they are mentioned. I could list famous sports figures with backgrounds from those countries whose temperament and character are compared to Stan, Mike Krzyzewski, or Jim Furyk, and the relation of the person to the place would be different and more positive.

So, there is good linkage and bad linkage. What determines the status of the linkage? Pondering Pole theory: there is linkage based upon at least one defining factor that influences and "convinces" a person that upon hearing the word will register a positive response. I picked the countries mentioned in the previous paragraph because they signify three different linkage types. The first is "in your face," the second is "the big dude," and the third group is the "small dude with the big dude attitude." These six countries have various degrees of beautiful countryside, cuisine, famous places, and notable histories. How we think of them varies.

Italy in most respects has it all: the great history, a beautiful countryside, and famous places. Mexico has beautiful beaches and renowned archeological sites but the thing that set both countries apart and shines most favorably with Americans is the food. It is a tangible and direct path, an absolute "in your face" (and in your stomach) impression of these two nations and the reinforcement occurs millions of times a day, all over the country. Not sure how many pizzas and tacos are consumed each day, but it is a lot. Tummy feels good and registers with the brain when it comes to Italy and Mexico.

Russia and England have numerous famous places and are steeped in history but certainly don't have the reference to food as strongly as Italy and Mexico. The defining factor of these two countries is the powerful reputation they carry. The "big dude" with big shoulders like the largest kid in the class: you automatically respected him and wouldn't say anything bad about him because you did not want to get beat up. Sad, I guess, but true.

In the final category, two small nations, Ireland and Israel are the most intriguing. Both countries have interesting and famous historical sites, but they also have tricky weather and non-standard topography. Ireland is often rainy and cold, and Israel sits in the middle of a desert. Neither can boast a cuisine that is comparable to the variety and taste of Italian or Mexican. Neither has the power or reputation that England or Russia exudes. Yet, I find that the Irish and the Jewish as well as the non-Irish and non-Jewish can speak freely and confidently in near glowing terms about these two countries. Why so glowing?

It is all about will. Simply put, the Irish and Jewish do not tolerate any negativity from those outside the group and they also promote and market themselves well. They condition those around them to think highly of their ancestral land. I hear Irish or Jewish comedians laugh about themselves and their culture, but I don't hear too many others "kid" them about being Irish or Jewish (or being stupid) mainly because they do not allow it.

So, what linkage category do we fall into? Can the Poles get linkage from the food? Probably not, although the jury is still out, and we have nothing to be ashamed of in this area. Can Poles get linkage with English power and Russian reputation? Historically the Poles have had their empires and domineering moments but nothing as sustained and on par with those two giants, or China, Germany, Spain, or Persia for that matter. Our option is to create connections between people and place based on the Irish and Israeli model.

Every country's music, dance, food, history, and land will have some credibility, specialness, and beauty. The grace and blessings that God has bestowed on the Polish people has been very generous. On balance the people are good and decent and so is where they came from. We can sit around like the salesmen in David Mamet's *Glengarry Glen Ross* and hope someone gives us the "good leads," or we can stand up and get the positive linkage ourselves. Write the radio station, correct the speaker, or bring some delicious pastry to the Easter dinner and tell the folks straight up, well, this is Polish.

THE PONDERING POLE 2   2020–2023 and "BEST OF"

Brought me to tears.

Chris Botti is a world renown jazz trumpet player, and he performed a concert at Powell Symphony Hall in midtown St. Louis February 23rd. Chris's mean horn playing, combined with his outstanding accompanying band members, the special guests, Powell's orchestral background, along with the excellent acoustics made for a spectacularly satisfying evening. Then came the linkage.

Towards the end of the first half of the concert, Chris went into a short intro as he did with all the works played that night. He spoke about the fourteen consecutive visits the band had made to Poland and how much the Poles were enamored with jazz. Then he described his reasoning behind the next piece, his interpretative take on Frederick Chopin's °*Prelude in C Minor*.

Then came the tears. The gentle and sincere comments about Poland and the glorious jazz rendition of classical Chopin was a wonderful testament to the composer and to the Polish people and made my eyes well up. *That* was a connection between person and place, big time, and with a big heart. Linkage, yes, and dzienkuje bardzo Chris.

I want to wish all the Polish American Journal readers a happy and blessed Easter, Wesolego, Alleluja!

May 2013

"The Eagle Unbowed."

Look closely at the picture of the Polish soldiers on the cover. Focus on the sad and exhausted face of the marching young man peering directly at the camera. He is Henry, Charlie, and Joe. He is me. He is you. I have seen that face a hundred times. He is us.

Albin Wozniak, publisher of the Polish Studies Newsletter got it right in the February 2013 edition when he proclaimed, "Polonia should honor her for writing this book." The woman he refers to is Halik Kochanski and the book is *The Eagle Unbowed: Poland and the Poles in the Second World War* (Harvard University Press 2012). Buy as many copies as you can afford and give it to your children, grandchildren, to your friends, and then donate a copy to the neighborhood library. It is that good and important.

Here is why. The Polish experience is either non-existent, minimized, or put in a negative or biased light in popular culture such as movies and television and in our formal culture such as in our schools. Kochanski examines all the major parts of the war and gives the Polish perspective, whether it is good or not so good, but she gives a logical and clear picture of the context and circumstance surrounding whatever occurred. That is a refreshing thing and the mark of a stellar historian.

Another reason to read this history is to feel the power of both the sorrow and the incredible pressure the Poles lived under fighting to survive in truly unbelievable conditions in their country and abroad. We have heard so many times about how Poland "suffered" in World War II and this work illustrates that part of it. What is most satisfying to me was the dispelling or clarifying of what I thought was the history of the Polish performance on the battlefield and in diplomatic circles. In some cases *Eagle Unbowed* reveals information I was not aware of and with what I was familiar. The book often gave at least another take on those events, added a twist or two, and without passion.

The range of the historical record Ms. Kochanski presents is new and broad. World War II really began for the Poles as it had for many of the European nations from the end of World War I. Poland was a recovering and emerging entity and this had a tremendous impact materially and psychologically on how she would engage Germany and Russia when they attacked her September 1, and September 17, respectively, 1939. This, throughout the war, and until the "Final Chapter," the total war experience "left Poland devastated" (page 532).

There are several excellent books written about the Polish experience in World War II. Add this one to that list and please read it. Then consider as a meditation sometime during May, Polish freedom month, first that the Poles lost their freedom for over one hundred years, that their country was trashed and raped by the warring powers in World War I, that they fought *five* wars following World War I to secure their borders, that they worked very hard to build a nation between the wars only to see it destroyed because they *fought* Hitler and the Germans in the Second World War. To the critics, yes, the Poles made mistakes, did not do as much as they should have, and on and on but they also were engaged in the fight, mostly by themselves, with spirit and determination, and on balance, made decisions and acted appropriately from start to finish.

For all of this then, can you easily trade away the honor and identity of your ancestral background? Again, see the face and look into the eyes of the young soldier on the cover of *Eagle Unbowed*. I hope you never forget it.

Suggestion from the Pondering Pole

I am listening to a woman of Mexican descent describe how her uncle gets the family together to make tamales. He has the family secret, and he wants the rest of them to learn how to make it like grandma did. I knew an Italian family that did the same thing with raviolis. How about your family getting together to make pierogis or Chruscikis? What a great way to pass down the "art" of your personal ethnic cooking and have fun with the cousins.

Question for May, does your family meet to make the family secret recipe? I would love to hear the story.

A very big dziekuje bardzo to my friend Jim "Jak" (for Jakub) Rygelski for the wonderful gift of *Eagle Unbowed*. I also recommend you make the blueberry cheesecake from the *Mala Cukierenka* website (http://www.malacukierenka.pl/sernik-na-zimno-z-jagodami.html). Hint: there are equivalency websites out there for the amounts and use only an ounce of gelatin. It makes it fluffier and is absolutely delicious. Thank you, Susie, for making it for me.

August 2013

"Making" Tamales and Golabkis.

I received a wonderful eMail from Ed Drobinski referring to the May 2013 "Pondering Pole" talking about the Mexican uncle who brought the family together each year to make a batch of tamales using "grandma's" recipe. For additional background, none of the children in this Mexican family were married to anyone of Mexican descent. Eventually part- or non-Mexicans will be charged with the responsibility to preserve the tradition of making and eating these heritage tamales.

The connection to Ed was how his non-Polish wife Sue, learned to make pierogis and golabkis (cabbage rolls) from his grandmother. No written instructions and apparently babci (like all babcis) made them very well as requests come in regularly for Sue to create the Polish food. She is the family expert. The real triumph, as with the Mexican folks, is that it is not solely about the food that draws everyone in, but it is the fun and fellowship in preparing and eating it that makes it taste so great.

> *... and my grandmother wasted little time teaching Sue how to make golabki and pierogi without written recipes. Since then, Sue is the go-to girl for Easter, Christmas, and anyone's desire for a Polish meal. We normally make the pierogi for Christmas on the Sunday after Thanksgiving, with numerous friends joining the family for camaraderie, samples, and a share of the finished product.*
>
> *Krupnik and/or Wisniowka somehow make an appearance, and the event really takes off! My mom (Polish) and Sue's mom both take part as well. Sue has long since written down the recipes and shares them willingly, but we usually insist on a "making" party to show the technique.*

The "making" party, according to Ed, includes teaching the kids how to make grandma's golabek and introducing them to the Polish dish. This is one, but my hope is that there are a million stories out there like it. Teach a kid to make pierogi and you might be producing a future president of the Kosciuszko Foundation, the president of Poland, or the president of the United States. I believe it.

The Alluring Agnes B

I am sitting at the hairdresser's waiting for my shampoo and cut, and I picked up a copy of *Allure* magazine. If you are wondering, I was too lazy to walk over and pick up a copy of UFC (Ultimate Fighting Championship). After paging through the latest "trends," I noticed the Vice-President and publisher of *Allure* is Agnes Bogdan Chapski. "Bogdan" is how her name is listed on the staff page in the magazine otherwise she is Agnes B. Chapski everywhere else.

Back in the 2008 April edition of *"The Pondering Pole"* Klara Glowczewska was featured as the editor of *Conde' Nast Traveler*. *Allure* and *Traveler* are owned by Conde' Nast Publications and apparently, they like Polish girls as editors and publishers of their popular magazines. If you are a Polish woman, seek employment with Conde' Nast. They like you; they really like you.

Signage

In July of 2006, *"The Pondering Pole"* asked the question on how important it is to have Polish names or words for famous places and popular events. Seeing and hearing the Polish name or word resonates a positive vibe over and over. Sometime in the distant future, some young person will wonder, who was that person that bridge is named after and who were the ancestors? So now we have the new *Stan Musial Veterans Memorial Bridge* being built over the Mississippi River in St. Louis and I could not be happier. This is a tribute to Stan and excellent signage (until they rename it) for Polonia.

September 2013

You go Oprah!

I was surprised to hear a story about a very special and revered Polish person. This person (it is now the year 2013) still finds the need to put himself and the Polish people down by jokingly portraying them as backwards or stupid. What a shame but more than that, the question is how he should be treated compared to those non-Poles that denigrate the Polish people as backwards or stupid. One we call a bigot and the other – what? Confused? Treat him the same or treat him different? "Don't ever go against the family," the Godfather said. So how do you handle this situation?

About the same time and along the same lines, Oprah Winfrey announced that she does not tolerate hearing the "N" word in her presence. "You cannot be my friend and use that word around me," she declared. Using it would be anyone *including* other African Americans. There is the theory that African Americans may use the "N" word because they "lived" it, but non-African Americans may not. "Living it" has a different connotation for Oprah and most of the comments I am seeing and hearing have the public (excluding rappers, gangbangers, and professional African American athletes) admiring her courage and stand.

Finally, I am talking with someone at a party, and she spots a woman who, let's say at the least, is behaving badly. The person said, "I know this sounds terrible, but I cannot find it in my heart to forgive her. I cannot stand to be around her." Now, I am no saint by any means, but as a Catholic and a Christian, those words strike a chord. The human part of me wants to punish and ostracize, yet in another sense, to say "I will not forgive" hurts my ears. It is hard to do, forgive, but if you are a member of the club (Christian), it is integral for the believer.

Is it hypocritical then to condemn those outsiders who tell the Polish jokes or demean us to our faces, yet give a pass to those in our immediate or "extended" (any Polish person in the world) family who does the same? At least one way family is different because it goes against logic and science for a person to put himself down unless he has an inferiority complex, is ignorant, is fearful, or has some kind of self-loathing psychological condition.

Those outside the family might have the same or similar issues but they also have an agenda and a more perverse psychology. For those outside the group, there is a more powerful feeling that they are trying to harm us and that makes it unique. However, like both, my attitude towards them does not extend to enabling or acceptance. Like the immature and misguided children that they are, they must be taught that what they are doing is wrong and for what reason.

This brings us back to Oprah. She is powerful and independent, and she could easily crush the life out of the black person that referred to her as "a house n*****," or she could have blinked and yuck-yucked the episode to fit in with all the other people in *her* hood. Instead, she turned it around and used the incident as a teaching moment to simply tell those within and outside the group (and Spike Lee) what she really thinks is the right thing to do. My guess is that it is not necessarily what the hip-hoppers wanted to hear.

Evaluate the bad behavior (whether family or not), make a tough choice (as Oprah has done), and now the final and even harder part. For non-Poles that are mean to us, we forgive them but impress upon them that we will not enable them nor accept their bad behavior. For Poles, we should forgive them but similarly not enable them nor accept their bad behavior either. We call dealing with family members in critical situations tough love and there are various ways to do that.

Forgiveness is a key part of tough love but so is learning from the experience and that adds in a dash of hope. That is why saying "I will not forgive" is too harsh. There is always an opportunity to learn from a mistake and there is the hope that a person's behavior can be turned into something more positive and productive. Knowing Oprah as the upbeat person that she is and someone who has changed so many hearts and minds over the years, you must believe, if nothing else, she has the hope that she can make a difference hearing a bad word. I hope she does.

A Polka Encyclopedia?

Thanks to James Pula for completing the Polish American Encyclopedia. I have a copy and it is quite an impressive book. If you want to order one, it is

THE PONDERING POLE 2   2020–2023 and "BEST OF"

published by McFarland & Company, Inc., Publishers, Box 611, Jefferson, North Carolina 28640. To place an order by phone, call 800-253-2187.

For the next project, I would like to see an encyclopedia of Polka music in the United States including the words for some of our most famous and favorite polkas. A translation will be needed for those written in Polish. I was watching a Time-Life commercial about the Folk Music stars of the sixties and there aren't any Polish-Americans. Normally we have token representation and the lack of it for this genre dismayed me but then I thought about it and, hey, we made our own folk music during this time. His name was Eddie Blazonczyk and there were many others.

October 2013

A Tribute to the Polka Club.

Some hold each other tightly, some at a cautious distance. Some hold their arms out stiffly, some drop them loosely at their sides. Some dance springily, some glide softly, some move with grave dignity. There are boisterous couples, who tear wildly about the room, knocking everyone out of their way.

From *The Jungle* by Upton Sinclair

Mother taught me how to dance when I was a kid, and we danced the polka. So many of the weddings and parties near where she was born and raised in rural Southern Illinois were held at Sherman's Hall and it was there that she taught me how to stand, where to place my hands, and explained the steps and count. That place holds so many memories for me but especially as an introduction to the musical expressions of the Polish American polka. I owe her for that and for my love of dance in general. There is hardly a category or style I have not tried or can speak about or perform. It has given me so much enjoyment throughout my life to know about and be able to dance.

Polka and the accordion in this country, as it goes by extension of the "Polish" thing, get a bad rap. Some of your local rock DJs for some inexplicable reason will refer to it when making the comparison between what is cool and what is not. Inexplicable because rock and polka are not related. I cannot think of any other *folk music* that gets beat up as much. There is a note in the Bruce Springsteen biography, however, telling the story of when the E-Street band fronted the rock band *Chicago*. Peter Cetera (half Polish and half Hungarian) bassist-singer of *Chicago* entertained both bands at the backstage party playing "Polish music on Federici's accordion." Bruce "The Boss" Springsteen had an accordion player on stage with him at his concert this past March in Kansas City. Apparently accordion is okay for "The Boss."

THE PONDERING POLE 2   2020–2023 and "BEST OF"

> *And this is their utterance; merry and boisterous, or mournful and wailing, or passionate and rebellious, this music is their music, music of home.* **(The Jungle, page 11.)**

Life goes on and except for an occasional dance in college, a festival, or a wedding out in the country, I did not have a lot of contact or primary focus on polka and didn't think much about it. Mom and pop came "home" to polka during the "rise of the unmeltable" period during the late seventies and eighties. They found a group of polka lovers which accepted them, and they loved being with these folks. They were having a blast going to dances and traveling to exotic places with their club. They were happy and that made me happy for them. Then pop passed away.

It was during this time when I did some sub duty as my mom's dance partner and I met the group: Danny and Estelle, Charlie and Marcella, Ginny and Chester, Tom and Terri, Gene and Carolyn, Ted and Leona, Jack and Wanda, Ernie and Mary, and too many others to mention. I was shocked to discover that they abstained from drinking beer or other alcoholic beverages, discouraged excessive laughter and nonsense, and for sure, tried not to have any fun. Maybe I'm wrong on those things, but they could dance!

There is the quote that Ginger Rogers could do everything that Fred Astaire could do only in high heels and backwards and that certainly rings true for these women. The guys were solid leaders and got into it as much as the gals. The fluidity, the joy, and the skill they possessed as a group was wonderful to behold and was contagious. As mentioned, I know a little bit about what constitutes dancing, even good dancing, and they were good. So good that I had on occasion one or two beers with them and tried a few yips.

The polka club is still going but I constantly have to tell them to go faster! They yell back, "*you* go faster!" The bodies are slowing down and now it is life that is going by, faster and faster. So, *Na Zdrowie*, thank you, and I salute the polka club and for that matter, all the good friends, and times, and all the polka clubs in our country! Dancing is the good drug and if you are Polish, it is as much a part of you as breathing. Please, take your son or daughter or some young person out on the floor and teach them, "the steps and the count." Maybe it will be the start of a new polka club.

Read more about it!

There is a book on polka! It is an excellent book on polka called *Polka Happiness* by Charles Keil, Angeliki Keil, and Dick Blau, published in 1992. Here is a brief description of the book on the Amazon website (http://www.amazon.com/Polka-Happiness-Visual-Studies-Charles/dp/1566394627) where you can order it: "*Polka Happiness* captures the energy, excitement, and shared sense of belonging embodied in polka sociability." Sounds like a polka club perhaps?

Speaking of going home...

In the August 18th, 2013, issue of Parade magazine, there is an insert about actor John Krasinski's trip to Poland with his father "tracing his father's roots and relatives." Said John, "It was one of the most emotional experiences of my life." Really neat to see this and you can read the rest of the story at http://www.parade.com/ancestry.

Happy Polish Heritage Month and wishing you much *"Polka Happiness."*

December 2013

What was all the pondering about?

*F*or the record, this is the 99th installment of the Pondering Pole. To recognize and celebrate the occasion, I would ask that you indulge me so that for this edition, let's look back at the purpose and goal originally set forth for the column. Let us reminisce a little if you will. Then for number one hundred, I want to offer up some thoughts and ideas on what might be (might we) accomplished in 2014 and beyond. As always, let us explore and "ponder" together.

Way back in 2005 I wrote:

> *I am constantly amazed at how many persons or historical events have a Polish connection or twist I was not aware of and am pretty sure Polonia and certainly most Americans are not as well. While most of us are familiar with the "Cs," Curie, Chopin, and Copernicus… there are many lesser known but equally interesting and significant stories about how our people are involved and have contributed to this country and elsewhere throughout history.*

I should have said constantly amazed "to discover" some of the hidden stars and gems of Polonia, to look where no one else was looking and to research those people, events, and stories that many of us did not know or realize. Since the project was an immense undertaking, part of the plan was to engage others in the "work." This has truly been a success both in revealing new notable persons of Polish extraction and by exciting others of Polish extraction to join in the fun of the hunt. The final bonus of all this was that the research evolved towards analyzing and seeing more to the person or story than met the eye. Why became as important as who or what in this exercise. All the aspects of being a "Pondering Pole" became truly satisfying to me and it helped others to think about it as well.

So, over the last eight years I found out that Jim Furyk (future golf professional Hall-of-Famer), Peter Cetera of the rock group *Chicago* fame, Meg Ryan, Hollywood film star, and Ryan Newman, NASCAR driver are part Polish. That there is a Polish connection to the Enron scandal, with one of the "most influential writers" of Ireland (James Joyce), in the Broadway musical *West Side Story*, in "String Theory," "Intelligent Design," at The Matchbox bar in Chicago, with the television show *Flipper*, dancing the tango, film star Audrey Hepburn's ballet training, and with the movie, ready, *King Kong*! I became introduced to famous people such as Tamara de Lempicka (art deco painter), John Szarkowski (photographer), Zbigniew Rybczynski (music-video director), Stanislaw Wyspianski (renowned painter and contemporary of Henrik Ibsen, Gustav Klimt, and Paul Gauguin), and finally, Michael Sokolski, creator of Scantron, the multiple-choice testing method (Ugh!).

And, as they say in the commercials, there was "much, much more." For me, the most important thing in this long journey was the analysis and the lessons learned. That would be the "why" part previously mentioned and interspersed throughout. To my surprise, there was a profound Polish idea in the topic of economics, theology, arts and literature, psychology, and at least twenty times in history. The Polish soul, heart, mind, blessing, tomato, and Angel Wing were examined. I believe I can explain now why the people that love us, love us, and I am beginning to understand why the people that aren't seeking therapy (although, many most likely are.) The latter also might be simply a lost cause or fall into the category of prerequisite, psychology – insane. For the whole of it though, what I can tell you, become your own Pondering Pole. I hope you find it as fulfilling and satisfying as I do.

That's what I'm talking about!

Timing is everything. As substantiation for the 99th edition of the Pondering Pole, along comes a perfect gift. Gil Mros sends me an article he wrote for the Polish Genealogy Society of Minnesota (Summer 2013 pgs. 21-23) on the ancestral birthplace of Benjamin Kubelsky, aka, the comedian and television star, Jack Benny. Is he Polish or not?

To make a long story short, yes, he is. The remarkable and impressive thing though was the detective work involved in finding and compiling the list of clues that eventually led to that conclusion. Here is one example for starters: Benny's wife consistently claimed his family was from Lithuania. True but then perhaps he came from a Polish town in Lithuania. What was the primary language of the family? How should immigration and census records be interpreted?

On and on with these and many other questions and considerations, the why, who, and what just discussed. Eventually, when adding it all up, according to Gil, "I felt confident in stating that if Meyer Kubelsky (Jack's father) spoke Polish and came from Poland, then he was indeed Polish." Wikipedia and other sources for Benny's ancestral background can now be corrected. As the team at the research bureau of the Pondering Pole like to say in a case like this, cza-czing!

A heartfelt Wesolych Swiat to all the Polish American Journal readers, advertisers, and staff. I am especially grateful to all the folks that read the Pondering Pole, those that I have corresponded with, and those that have helped or contributed in any way for the last eight years. Dziekuje bardzo to you and joy and blessings at Christmas.

VII
2014

January 2014

So now what?

Way back in the January 2013 edition of the Pondering Pole it was mentioned that we are in the last leg of the hundred-year immigration experience. That it takes a hundred years to "complete" the journey from ancestral homeland to where the children and grandchildren of the immigrants become fully integrated and ingrained in the new country and society.

A year later and it is fitting that for the 100th edition of the Pondering Pole, we discuss and "ponder" what is to become of the American Polish experience in the remaining 25 years of the journey. Since I don't know of an existing template for this kind of thing, here is a proposal: what does our Polish presence look like today, why are we doing this, and what are the goals and how do we accomplish them?

While my rich involvement with the American Polish community has always allowed for variation, the difference was primarily timing: the immigrants and their children lived from the early and middle part of the twentieth century, many Poles came after World War II as displaced persons, they came after the Solidarnosc revolution in the eighties, and they have trickled in as professionals from modern Poland looking for work, opportunity, and affluence. While their perspectives were somewhat diverse, the defining and unifying feature of all these movements was that they were fully Polish. They were totally Polish in the sense that they understood and claimed Polish culture and, in many cases, the Polish language, first.

The variation is still there but today's younger Polonia has taken on a different character and approach. The new Polish American can be defined primarily by his or her nature. It is not so much a question of when or how the person got here; the question is whether they claim to be Polish, or not. Polish people in the United States can be grouped in four categories: they are living it, they promote Polish and Poland, they are casual observers and participants, or they are not interested.

THE PONDERING POLE 2   2020–2023 and "BEST OF"

It is true that real Polish people still live in the United States. They assume and claim the culture and speak the language. They are Polish first in no uncertain terms just like all immigrants throughout the twentieth and twenty-first centuries. Promoters like being Polish so much that they retain a tie to the culture by working at the event, having membership at the church and attending Mass, making the food, and still have associations with other Poles. While Polish is a significant part of their lives, it is not the primary focus. America is not their adopted country; it is their country.

The casual observer will pay respects to the past and ancestry by occasionally participating with the community. This is an exercise in fun and reminiscing but the effort is a small part of their lives. They are 10 per centers at best. The final group, the largest, will most likely be mixed-Polish by parentage, or they might carry a Polish name, or even be a recent immigrant but have no inclination to acknowledge or exist as a Polish person. It is just not important to them as it is not important to most Americans. With this kind of mix, what can American Polonia aspire to going forward? Why are we doing this?

The "whys" I would summarize with three "Ls": legacy, livelihood, and love. As mentioned many times over the years in the Pondering Pole, Polish does not get the props (proper respect) or the press other ethnic groups do. The awareness of who we are and what we have accomplished is many times diminished. Bolstering and promoting our legacy then is a worthy and needed reason. And if how we are viewed by others is less than acceptable, then improving the attitude and perception of others towards us can only help to sweeten our livelihood such as with our jobs, in school, in the community, and in our relationships with friends and family. Finally, if there is a place in our heart for Polish culture, history, and background merely because we love it, shouldn't that by itself constitute enough motivation for promoting Polonia? And by extension, if you love something or someone, don't you want others to feel the same way? The truth is, for some of us, we are Polish and we love it and that is why we live it, promote it, and participate in it.

So we know who the players are and we know why we do it. Now the big, big question for January (and I invite you think long and hard about this yourself): How can we accomplish what we want to see continue and endure?

A standard answer is we *need* more of this and more of that and certainly we do. We need more livers, contributors, promoters, and more participators. We need to cover the bases like stocking the libraries with Polish-themed books, finding folks to take over when we are gone, and preserving the places we hold dear. Yes, we need people and covered bases and that is a good outcome. Rather than concentrate on the numbers though, I feel like we should focus more on the method and approach and the numbers and assurances will come. In all the cases where I have observed that a "new" Polish person has come on board, there was a transformation in their view of Polonia and then they became transformed.

To know thyself is one of the great purposes and experiences for a human being and introducing a Polish person to their heritage is a great way to start. A friend told me she gives the Polish American Journal to her nephew each month and that small bit of information made my day. He didn't have to read it but if it wasn't given to him, if it wasn't even near him, he wouldn't have had the chance to be transformed. I have seen this repeatedly with young people introduced to Polish dance, the festival, or cooking the food. The tangible, real, personal interaction, I believe, makes the difference.

Being Polish is not a religious experience (though that can be debatable) and I don't want this to sound like joining a cult but with as fast as the world is moving, with all the changes we are experiencing, with how technical the world is becoming, with how artificial our everyday lives are, learning about the sights, sounds, and smells of an ethnic culture, our culture, is a great way to stay in *touch* with humanity. We hear about the void that lies with the young people in our society. I believe one way that it can be filled is by self-awareness and meaning that is found through an understanding of your ethnicity. Ask someone to join you; invite somebody into your world. If you can influence one other person, no matter if she or he is 100% or 0% Polish to appreciate it as you do, then I have hope that Polonia will continue and endure.

Polish or Not?

Fascinating find on the EthniCelebs website (http://ethnicelebs.com). Juliette Binoche, the famous award-winning French actress and star of Krzysztof Kieslowski's *Three Colors: Blue*, has a partial Polish background and an amazing story. According to EthnicCelebs:

Juliette's mother was born in Częstochowa, Poland. Juliette's maternal grandfather was of Belgian (Walloon) and French descent, and Juliette's maternal grandmother was of Polish ancestry. Juliette's maternal grandparents, who were Catholic, were imprisoned at Auschwitz because they were considered to be intellectuals by the Nazi occupiers. Juliette's maternal grandparents were active in the theatre.

As mentioned last month, I am very grateful to all the folks that read the Pondering Pole, to those that I have collaborated and corresponded with, and those that have contributed in any way toward producing the 100 issues I have been blessed to write. Sto lat!, dziekuje bardzo, and good luck in 2014.

April 2014

Lenten meditation.

The country's second largest Mardi Gras celebration is in full swing here. I'm watching the parade and observing the young people around me, with delight and envy. I am positive that when I was in that perfect wheelhouse of age (25 to 35), strength, and beauty I did not have near the confidence and boldness that I witnessed that day. My wish for the young people is that they will appreciate and cherish these days of frivolity and mirth and at one point understand that along with life's parades come responsibility, opportunity, challenges, and sometimes a string of beads across the forehead.

So, I am watching these exceptional young people flit around and my thoughts turn to what is exceptional, who has it, and where do you get it. We hear about exceptionalism as it applies to the United States, talked about in liberal as well as in conservative circles. There are companies that have mission statements that include the word exceptional pertaining to service or products. Can we say that there is Polish exceptionalism? We have exceptional people and there have been examples of exceptional acts or behavior throughout Polish and Polish-American history.

Exceptionalism for country or company means going that extra length to satisfy or doing something in an extra special way. Cultures and cultural expression make it hard to be exceptional; rather it is expected and sufficient to just be. In that sense, all cultures are exceptional. I like the idea that we are what we are, but I also like to think we are sensitive to how we are thought of as individuals and as a group. An isolated group of people might be competitive with one another but not necessarily to those outside of the community.

The American experience is unique because there are so much mixing of peoples and traditions and whether apparent or not, the comparisons are there. Don't want to be selling Polish as exceptional all the time but I hope we are trying to be exceptional every time we are Polish. This is a point worth noting but hard to do. What do you think?

Paczki, a "jelly donut on steroids"

A well-known and popular DJ in St. Louis described paczki as "jelly donuts on steroids." Yes, that is so true and my addiction to these Polish drug-like pastries is exacerbated during Lent when they are so good and prevalent. Back to the parade, a Pondering Pole question for many years is why we don't 1) have a Polish float associating Zapusty with the French "Laissez Le Bon Temps Rouler" (Let the good times roll!), while 2) advertising paczki (perhaps even handing them out rather than the beads).

If not a float, then how about a paczki and coffee/hot coco stand? That would be an excellent choice for a cool or brisk March morning before or during the festivities especially for those not slurping down beer or bourbon, though you could offer a coffee and bourbon option for those that prefer the royale. If you have a Fat Tuesday event in your city, include the paczki, mon ami, any way you can!

Polish or Not?

Cross off John Candy, comedian, and actor, on the Polish or not list!! (I knew it!) According to the Ethnic Celebs, (http://ethnicelebs.com/john-candy) he is Polish and Ukrainian on his mother's side though by the look of the names he most likely is all Polish from his mother but born in Ukraine.

On the 2014 Academy Awards "In Memoriam" list was Stefan Kudelski, inventor. In Wikipedia (http://en.wikipedia.org/wiki/Stefan_Kudelski) he was born in Warsaw and is "known for creating the Nagra audio (tape) recorders." Kudelski won the Oscar for Scientific or Technical award in 1965, 1977, and 1978.

June 2014

Delivery Man, *DreamWorks SKG and Touchstone Pictures*, 2013.

Okay, it wasn't just me that was anxious about the release of a new movie with Vince Vaughn, billed as a comedy, and with trailers showing obvious Polish accoutrements and symbols. Perhaps you will remember that Vince starred in a film with Jennifer Aniston called *The Break Up*, playing the main character Gary Grobowski (Gro?), a loser who is crude and backwards with women and in life, and ends the story with no redeeming value or possibility for success. You know, the "same old" Hollywood Polish thing.

The new movie produced and distributed in 2013 is called *Delivery Man*, and stars Vince Vaughn as David Wozniak, a delivery truck driver for the family meat processing business who we find out is a former fertility clinic donor whose "donations" produced 533 children of which 144 of those offspring sue the clinic to find out the identity of their father. With a storyline like that, with Vince Vaughn, billed as a comedy, and plenty of Polish accoutrements and symbols, well you might say as I did, yep, "same old thing."

Surprisingly, it is not. I think the Hollywood bigots had the perfect outline but forgot to read the script! As the legal process works itself out, David learns about himself, life, and what it means to connect and care for someone, or in this case 144 someones plus the woman he is having a baby with. I found myself watching and waiting and watching and waiting for the big one, the "same old" scene as in *The Break Up* where David does something crude, backwards, or irreparably stupid. Instead, I watched scene after scene building to a grand denouement of encouragement and positivity.

David Wozniak finishes the movie as a credible and sensitive guy and someone I liked, a lot. Don't be fooled, he does play the "problem child" of the family and his behavior is not always top-notch. That is the backdrop but woven around this flawed man is his family seen as solid and decent people and I especially loved how the Polish dad was portrayed and acted. I do recommend you see this movie and let me know what you think.

Polish or Not?

Robert Lamm, original founder, and performer in the rock band Chicago along with Jason Scheff, another Chicago alum, produced a CD for Polish singer/songwriter Zosia Karbowiak. Zosia's work is modern and quite good. Does Robert or Jason have any Polish in them or was their relationship with Zosia the result of Chicago (the city) osmosis?

From the July Pondering Pole, I said:

"For some time, I believed that Richie Sambora, the lead guitarist for the band was half Polish (mom). Ethnic Celebs (http://ethnicelebs.com) brings him in as 100% Polish but I would challenge the name Sambora as being Polish."

Received a very nice letter from Joseph Malon who lived near the Sambora's in the old neighborhood in Perth Amboy, New Jersey, and he confirms that Richie's dad Adam was 100% Polish. Now that is A+ Pondering Pole verification!

September 2014

An idea.

On the boats and on the planes
They're coming to America.
Never looking back again
They're coming to America.

They're Coming to America, by Neil Diamond

As this is written there is a flood of young children from Latin America crossing the southern border of the United States. While there is a lot of talk about the reason for their coming and the humanitarian nature of caring for the kids most of the debate is over immigration policy and the ramifications of this kind of "invasion." Considering all the aspects of this event and politics aside, can *any* Polish American not empathize or sympathize or at the least consider this latest mass migration to the United States? For good or bad, what is happening on our Southern border should be familiar to us all. Been there, done that.

I have my own opinions on the proper course for our immigration policy but no matter what the reasoning, this immigration, part of the most recent of the four major U.S. immigrations makes me think of the many Polish migrations to the United States. To summarize U.S. immigrations briefly, the first major American influx was primarily British, the second occurred in the mid-19th century due to the great Irish famine, the third was the industrial revolution of the early 20th century bringing in low cost labor from Southern and Eastern Europe, and the most recent and familiar to us beginning in the 1960s is the influx of undocumented migrants from Mexico and more and more, from Latin America, Honduras, Guatemala, and El Salvador.

Polish immigration has four major segments beginning with very sparse entries in the mid and late 1800s, then the large influx in the early 20th century, continued with post World War II displacement, during martial law with the rise of the Solidarity movement, and as part of the general legal immigration policies of the United States government during and after.

The Poles that came here to work in the factories in the early 1900s were the original Mexicans. Many of our people worked here and then sent the money back home or went back home with some dollars in their pockets. As humble and hard working as I believe my grandfather was when he came over on the boat, somehow, he was able to own some farmland in the countryside outside of the city. If Mexicans and other Latin Americans are doing the jobs Americans won't do, then the Poles, Italians, and Slovaks apparently were doing it in 1925 as well.

October 2014

Maestro.

There are two sides to this story, and it is the sum of them that makes it significant and interesting. The first part is the accomplishment of the man and the second is the legacy. Karol Lipinski was a contemporary, friend, and rival of Niccolo Paganini, who is considered by many (based on how often he appears at the top of many of the lists) as the greatest violin player of all time. The Lipinski legacy is the type of Stradivarius violin with his name attached to it.

The best source I can find about the history of the man and the legacy is an excellent online article and chapter called *A Violin's Life, The Lipinski Stradivarius* (http://aviolinslife.org/lipinski/). After reading *A Violin's Life* and learning about the wonderful life of Karol Lipinski, I am slightly surprised there is not more awareness about him. Though this is dated, in the book, *Paganini*, by Renee de Saussine (McGraw-Hill, New York, 1954) there are a grand total of three pages that mention Lipinski. Geoffrey Seitz, a well-known violin maker in St. Louis was not familiar with the Lipinski Stradivarius. However, I did receive this eMail response from another violin maker, Robert Clemens who said:

> *Yes, I make a Guarneri model violin after the Lipinski Guarneri as referred to by my teacher who was acquainted with the original as a member of a large Chicago violin shop many years ago. This is my most sought-after design and sounds exceptional. The Lipinski Strad (a different instrument) was in the news recently as it was stolen and then recovered in the Milwaukee area.*

Born in 1790 in Radzyn, Poland, Karol Lipinski grew up in a musical family during the turmoil of the nation's partitions. His eventual playing style as a violist became purely classical and the road he took in achieving notoriety and success was in the classical way as well. The Lipinski family was employed by the Potocki aristocratic estate and after the total partition of

Poland they lost their stipend. Karol's father Felix had to scramble, make adjustments, and work very hard to live and support his family. Karol's big break came when his father allowed him to lead a chamber ensemble in the city of Lwow where "musical life flourished."

It was in Lwow that Karol's talents began to emerge, and the responsibility learned and experience he gained infused him with more confidence and social bearing. He flourished and others began to take notice. An Austrian by the name of Ferdinand Kremes became his mentor and steered him toward making the violin his primary instrument and sole interest. Lipinski took Kremes' advice and immersed himself in the study and pursuit of everything violin and based on the suggestion of one of the outstanding violinists of the time, another Austrian, Louis Spohr, decided to strike out on his own to pursue a career as a solo performer.

To say that Lipinski's career had a classic structure and direction is evident by the number of logical and measured steps taken in his personal and professional life. He progressively became better off for each new stage of development than in the previous. At one point then it was natural for him to go to the highest point and there was Niccolo Paganini. As I read it, Lipinski pursued Paganini to understand the man as well as experience his brilliance. In 1817, he toured Italy and met with Paganini and became friends with him. Then:

> *On April 17, 1818, they appeared in the packed theater of Piacenza. They played Kreutzer's 'Concerto for two violins and orchestra' and some of their own compositions to a very enthusiastic house. A second duo concert followed, and Paganini suggested a joint tour of Italy. Lipinski, however, was anxious about his wife, who was expecting a baby, and decided to return home. A few weeks later Paganini, writing to a friend, commented that the Pole had "… played my quartets … truly excellently." Lipinski, while enjoying and admiring Paganini's showy virtuosity, decided to remain faithful to the more classic style he had derived from Spohr.*

It was Lipinski's involvement with Paganini that drew him to a connection in Milan, the student of the master violinist Tartini by the name of Signor Salvini. Salvini's appraisal of his playing and the devotion to the classical style impressed him so much that he cried basta! (No more!), and asked him to meet on the next day. Lipinski played for him and at one point Salvini grabbed his violin out of his hands and smashed it over a table. Salvini gave him another to replace it and thus begat the legacy.

> *"I took it, and after I had played one of Beethoven's sonatas, Salvini extended his hand to me and deeply moved said: 'You probably know that I was a pupil of Tartini's. It was he who, on one occasion, gave me this grand, original Stradivarius of which I take great care in honor of his memory. You are the only one who knows how to handle this instrument to elicit from it all the beauty hidden inside.'*
>
> *'But,' I exclaimed, 'here lives the world famous Paganini!'*
>
> *'Don't mention his name in front of me,' the furious old man angrily shouted. 'I have heard this charlatan play on one string with no musical depth whatsoever; but is it possible to dazzle listeners solely with technical feats, without producing a genuine, full, round tone? Paganini may be admired, but you're playing thrills and moves everyone. You are following in the footsteps of Tartini and therefore, please accept this violin as a gift from me and at the same time as a memento of Tartini.'"*
>
> *Lipinski would play this violin, the not-yet-named-Lipinski Strad, for the rest of his life.*

What an amazing person Karol Lipinski! What a life! There are so many lessons that can be learned from his story and so much to be impressed with. Although the music school in Wroclaw Poland is named after him, and violin sellers like Robert Clemens know him I wish his name and works were better known. He is a great example for artistic passion and professional determination and, I believe, a super solid model of the human character. Spread the word!

November 2014

There was a time...

I have written before about the importance of ethnic naming in a multi-national country like the United States. There is Germantown, Illinois, Dublin, Ohio, and New Prague, Minnesota. There is also Sandusky, Ohio, and Pulaski County in just about every state in the union. I like that and since we have a Warsaw in Missouri, I was curious about how it came to be named.

According to the official website of Warsaw, Missouri, it is believed the town was named Warsaw in honor of Tadeusz Kosciuszko, revolutionary hero of the United States and of Poland. They're not sure though. From the history section on the city website, "There is no written record of how the name "Warsaw" was chosen, however, street names are mostly patriotic and it is believed that the name, which was the capital city of Poland, was chosen in honor of the Polish Patriot Kosciuszko" (http://www.welcometowarsaw.com/23/Our-History). Of course, there is a story behind every story and so we wonder why *this* patriot was chosen when there were so many others available with all those cultural backgrounds more like the inhabitants of the area in which the city rests. Perhaps the person leading the search wanted something different or unique. Wouldn't you love to meet *that* guy?

From Warsaw, Missouri and across the state to the other side of the Mississippi lies Warsaw, Illinois. I came upon this Warsaw while reading, *American Crucifixion, The Murder of Joseph Smith and the Fate of the Mormon Church*, by Alex Beam (Public Affairs, New York, 2014). This is a well written book about a fascinating subject, and I recommend it. Warsaw was the downstream neighbor and competitor to Nauvoo, Illinois, the Joseph Smith newly created home of the Mormons after they had been chased out of Ohio and Missouri. The Warsavians kept a suspicious eye on the activities and beliefs of the Mormon contingent.

The people of Warsaw, Illinois, at that time more Westerners than Midwesterners, most likely kept a suspicious eye on the activities and beliefs of all the people coming through, some staying and many others going North,

West, or South. As queer as the Mormons were to them, the thought had to occur to all or some of them why their town was called Warsaw and not some English, Scottish, or Irish sounding name. At least one, John Hay (who would grow up to become Abraham Lincoln's personal secretary and later, secretary of state), wondered why the name was changed from Fort Edwards and then Spunky Point said,

> "I lived at Spunky Point on the Mississippi river." Hay later wrote,
>
> "So named because some Indian rode by Fort Edwards on a spunky horse. This is a graphic and characteristic title of geographical significance, but some idiots just before I was born, who had read Miss Porter's novel "Thaddeus of Warsaw," thought Warsaw would be more genteel, so we are Nicodemussed [reduced by timidity] into nothingness for the rest of time.
>
> I hope every man who is engaged in this outrage is called Smith in heaven."

Reading this opinion on the validity and worth of the town's name I am betwixt between a good and bad impression. Though Mr. Hay felt distressed that the name Warsaw is common or boring, conversely, and apparently there were some that held a high regard for the imagery and distinction of that place. In addition, my reaction was to wonder what the heck "Thaddeus of Warsaw" is all about.

Overall, I was tickled with the idea of "Miss Porter" (Jane Porter the author of the book) thinking that the Warsaw of "Thaddeus of Warsaw" was a typical European enclave containing healthy amounts of "genteel" culture and society. In those days then, Warsaw could be thought of as more sophisticated at least in Jane Porter's mind than any American city. Here is a brief description of "Thaddeus of Warsaw" from Wikipedia (http://en.wikipedia.org/wiki/Thaddeus_of_Warsaw):

> **Thaddeus of Warsaw** was an 1803 novel written by Jane Porter. It comprised four volumes and was a groundbreaking work of historical fiction, "arguably the first English historical novel". The story was

derived from eyewitness accounts of British soldiers and Polish refugees fleeing the failed revolts against the foreign occupation of Poland in the 1790s…

Porter wrote that her goal was "to exhibit so truly heroic and enduring a portrait of what every Christian man ought to be"; she felt obliged to look at the past and to Poland because such people were "extinct" within Britain in her time.

I have not read "Thaddeus of Warsaw", but I did read some of the reviews of this book on Amazon and I am further encouraged to get a copy. This one by "Song Sparrow," "… it'll really pull you around emotionally. It's a great story, great history and of course a lot of treachery and tragedy. I really enjoyed it". If you read "Thaddeus of Warsaw" please share your thoughts about the book.

Refreshing isn't it, that there is a lovely little river town called Warsaw, Missouri, a lovely little river town called Warsaw, Illinois, and a historical Gothic Romance novel called "Thaddeus of Warsaw." I don't think it is popular to name places or cities after famous European or worldly cities anymore but the irony of this is the very word Warsaw, today, in the United States elicits a much different reaction than Jane Porter could imagine. It is 2014 and I believe we are going backwards. That's a shame, isn't it?

December 2014

Talki Polski

> I was tryin' to find my way home,
> but all I heard was a drone.
>
> Bouncing off a satellite; crushin' the
> last lone American night.
>
> This is radio nowhere, is there anybody alive out there?
>
> From *Radio Nowhere* by Bruce Springsteen

*T*alk radio and talk television are big. There is news and news analysis, television entertainment magazines, social commentary, and political potpourri daily. We are inundated with it. If you are a junkie, it can overwhelm your rehab and resistance. For the all the criticism of the shouting, debating, and fighting, we really are lucky to have so much information freely available. For me, TV and radio talk fit nicely into my regimen for keeping up on current affairs and it actually provides a good dose of relaxation and revelry. It sometimes becomes a drone, but I like it.

Since I have so many hours and so much intellectual stock invested in listening to and watching talk shows and since everything I do morphs into an ethnic face I am continually listening and watching for Polish participation in this great American phenomenon. If it is important and popular, I am hoping (or expecting) someone of the Polish or Slavic race to be part of it. In this case, I wish there were more ski's, ich's, and wicz's. Here are a few names to start you wishing.

> *Laura Ingraham – conservative talk show host and frequent contributing guest on many network political shows, Ingraham's mother is Polish. I once heard her talk about it and she indicated she was "proud" to be Polish.*

A graduate of Dartmouth College, a lawyer, and the author of many books, Laura is tough and outspoken.

Mika Brzezinski – daughter of the former National Security Advisor and scholar Zbigniew Brzezinski and co-host of MSNBC's Morning Joe. *She has authored a number of books and is generally left leaning in her political views.*

Adam Andrzejewski – Adam "Angie-f-ski" (yes, that was at least one translation found and not bad) appeared in a John Stossel feature about government "Overlords," politicians who demonstrate privilege by being excessive spenders of tax funds for themselves. (Some would call this stealing.) Besides owning a business, he is the founder of the government watchdog website www.openthebooks.com. Adam is a well-spoken individual and presents himself nicely on camera. Keep your eye on him. I hope he gets many more contributing guest (or better) host opportunities in the future.

Katie Pavlich – Katie is a beautiful Slavic but non-Polish young lady with personality and smarts to match. She appears frequently as a contributing guest analyst on Fox News *Hannity and* The Five. *She is a journalist and is the author of a couple books, all this before the ripe old age of 27. Need to clone Katie a thousand times across the American Eastern European spectrum.*

Elizabeth Hasselbeck – nee Filarski (father), sat in the conservative seat alongside the liberal chairs on The View. *A feisty debater and a fighter for her beliefs in* The View *crowd, she has moved up to be a co-host on* Fox & Friends. *To her credit, Elizabeth Hasselbeck is a survivor. I hope we have her presence on television for a long time to come.*

Let me know if I have missed anyone.

2014

Mr. Mizzou

Last year Missouri lost a favored son when Stan Musial went to the great Sportsman's Park in the sky. This year the Missouri Tiger football program lost their beloved coach, known affectionately as "Mr.Mizzou," with the loss of John Kadlec. I know John is Polish because forty years ago he told me he was.

I was introduced to him during a visit to my high school senior year after I had expressed interest in playing football for Mizzou. After he viewed my game films and we talked, he asked, "What kind of name is that?" "Yeah," he said, "I'm Polish too." It ended up all I was offered was a walk-on slip but that short, small talk exchange, and his gentle manner, made me like him.

Except for hearing him as a commentator on the Tiger broadcasts and from an occasional interview, I did not know that much about him. Apparently, my impression was multiplied a million times over by players, students, friends, and fans. Here is an excerpt from the Columbia, Missouri, *Daily Tribune* that speaks to his legacy (http://www.columbiatribune.com/sports/tigerextra/mr-mizzou-john-kadlec-dies/article_d4ded6a3-09dd-51f2-a91b-3d39ab5385f4.html).

> *"What you saw is what you got. Just a genuine good, good man."*
>
> *Kadlec, who usually wore a smile, was a beloved figure in the state. He connected the Missouri football eras from Don Faurot to Gary Pinkel. The St. Louis native was an all-conference lineman for Faurot in the 1940s; an assistant under Faurot, Frank Broyles, Dan Devine and Al Onofrio through the 1977 season; an athletic administrator at MU beginning in the 1980s; and the analyst for football radio broadcasts for 16 years beginning in 1995.*
>
> *"He was an ambassador for the University of Missouri his whole life and certainly his last years," Pinkel (Current Tiger coach Gary Pinkel) said. "I was fortunate to be around him. He had a huge influence on all his players. Thousands of players, I've seen them at reunions, these guys just embrace him. I feel so fortunate and blessed to have a guy like that in my life. We're going to miss him dearly."*

THE PONDERING POLE 2   2020–2023 and "BEST OF"

The testimonials about him are high and heartfelt and he will be missed. Whether he would have realized it or not and for all the people John Kadlec helped, simply by his life and example he did so much on behalf of the Polish people. Dzienkuje Bardzo "Mr. Mizzou" and rest in peace.

For the Polish Secret Santa

Here is a fun gift for the outdoors person in your life especially one with a Polish pedigree. The longtime cartoonist for the Missouri Conservationist magazine is Betty Chmelniak Grace (a Buffalo, New York girl for your – information!) has a new book out, a collection of over 200 of her cartoons called *Outside Jokes*. $8.75 and you can order it toll free 877-521-8632 or visit the e-commerce site at mdcnatureshop.com.

Wesoly Swiat to all Polish American Journal friends and subscribers. I truly hope you have a joyful, holy, family oriented, and Polish filled Christmas and holiday season.

VIII
2015

January 2015

Achievers and Greasers.

Unfortunately for me, the things that stick in my craw will remain there until I can find resolution and solace. That is why I always have a bottle of Tums at my side.

In the "Quotes" section of the Polish American Journal in July of 2014 there was an excerpt from the show *The Millers* where the character Carol Miller said, "Poland is ahead of the U.S. in math and science. Poland?" If we knew that Carol was Polish and was a fan of Polish that questioning could have been a reasonable expression of surprise and support for the small country that is better at something than the large country. In this case, let's be real, *The Millers* is a comedy, out of Hollywood, and well, not so much. Humor at our expense and it sticks in my craw.

However, since I am a super positive guy, I will ignore *The Millers* aspersions and interpret that comment as, yes but no surprise, small country is better than large country, in this case in math and science. I decided to research *The Millers* math and science reference and was pleasantly surprised. Be careful of interpreting the stats but there seems to be a lot of evidence that the Poles do very well in these two categories and are not too far down the list on the third big one, reading. See the charts below for instance.

THE PONDERING POLE 2   2020–2023 and "BEST OF"

Mathematics		Reading		Science	
Shanghai-China	613	Shanghai-China	570	Shanghai-China	580
Singapore	573	Singapore	542	Singapore	551
Chinese Taipei	560	Japan	538	Japan	547
Hong Kong-China	561	Hong Kong-China	545	Finland	545
Korea	554	Korea	536	Hong Kong-China	555
Liechtenstein	535	New Zealand	512	Australia	521
Macao-China	538	Finland	524	New Zealand	516
Japan	536	France	505	Estonia	541
Switzerland	531	Canada	523	Germany	524
Belgium	515	Belgium	509	Netherlands	522
Netherlands	523	Chinese Taipei	523	Korea	538
Germany	514	Australia	512	Canada	525
Poland	518	Ireland	523	United Kingdom	514
Canada	518	Liechtenstein	516	Poland	526
Finland	519	Norway	504	Ireland	522
New Zealand	500	Poland	518	Liechtenstein	525
Australia	504	Netherlands	511	Slovenia	514
Estonia	521	Israel	486	Switzerland	515
Austria	506	Switzerland	509	Belgium	505
Slovenia	501	Germany	508	OECD average	501
Viet Nam	511	Luxembourg	488	Chinese Taipei	523
France	495	United Kingdom	499	Luxembourg	491
Czech Republic	499	OECD average	496	Viet Nam	528
OECD average	494	Estonia	516	France	499
United Kingdom	494	United States	498	Austria	506
Luxembourg	490	Sweden	483	Czech Republic	508
Iceland	493	Macao-China	509	Norway	495
Slovak Republic	482	Italy	490	United States	497
Ireland	501	Czech Republic	493	Denmark	498
Portugal	487	Iceland	483	Macao-China	521
Denmark	500	Portugal	488	Sweden	485
Italy	485	Hungary	488	Italy	494
Norway	489	Spain	488	Hungary	494
Israel	466	Austria	490	Israel	470
Hungary	477	Denmark	496	Iceland	478
United States	481	Greece	477	Lithuania	496

From the Business Insider – December 3, 2013, "Here's the new ranking of top countries in Reading, Science, and Math" by Joe Weisenthal (http://www.businessinsider.com/pisa-rankings-2013-12).

Keep your eye out for the 2014 *Business Insider* and other reputable rankings that will most likely be published soon. The bottom line, and there is no boasting or "pride" here but merely another substantiation of something we knew all along – our people in Poland are well educated and do well in school and in the workplace.

Not me necessarily, but our people. This is true for our Polish people in Poland and the United States. For example, I recall that my class at William Cullen McBride High School, one of many Catholic prep schools in St. Louis back in the sixties was pretty smart. According to Father Piekarski, (Marianist priest and math teacher during the week), it was the grade just ahead of us that was most outstanding. The top-ten honor roll posts each quarter usually included three "skis." As I recall, one went on to become an engineer, one became an accountant, and one continued to be the great, lovable, and musical being that he always was and excelled at whatever endeavors he pursued.

I don't know what the statistics are for Polish American kids in education and scores compared to other ethnic groups, but I am thinking they are not too much different than their European counterparts. At least from the anecdotal evidence, I think we are doing ok.

"Like rama lamma lamma ka dinga da dinga dong"

There were greasers (or as we say in St. Louie, "greazers") at McBride and some were on the honor roll. The sixties and seventies were a strange transition time where some of us baby boomers drifted into the hippie scene and others clung to the black leather and the lure of the city. The lure of the city meant their families hadn't moved to the suburbs yet.

Most of us were confused and got by existing in one or the other world, a mix of the two, or in neither of them. Like the legend of the Polish math and science person, watching the movie *Grease* again made me remember McBride's greazers, the Broadway musical's greasers, and their Polish background.

Jim Jacobs is the co-creator of the musical theatre hit *Grease*, and I found an excellent online article from the Chicago Tribune featuring him talking about the origins (http://articles.chicagotribune.com/2011-04-22/entertainment/ct-ae-0424-grease-20110422_1_sandy-dumbrowski-grease-jim-jacobs) of the people, place, and culture that he based the play on. Jim got his inspiration from the kids at Taft High School on Chicago's Northwest side.

> *"Stop," he suddenly shouts on Normandy Avenue. "Sandy lived right there."*
>
> *A startled father and daughter in a front yard across the street disappear quickly into their home as we all pile out of the car to stare and take pictures of the modest frame house. I wonder to myself if they know they live right across the street from Sandy Dumbrowski.*
>
> *... Jacobs is talking about the real Sandy — a much-desired teenager called Jeanie Kozemczak, long gone from the area. She was Polish-American like most of the rest of the folks in a blue-collar neighborhood where Italian-Americans ran a*

> *close second, where most of the fathers had been in World War II and now worked factory jobs on Chicago's West Side.*

So the era of *Grease* and the kids at Taft that were part of it had names like Zuko (we had a Panko – not a greaser by the way) and Kenickie (Kaniecki) and at the center of it all was the beautiful Sandy Dumbrowski or as Jim Jacobs tells us, the real Sandy, the "much-desired" Jeanie Kozemczak. These people we watch with amusement in the musical *Grease* were our friends and relatives in many cases and they were part of our lives in an intimate way, or we observed them from afar. Quite the phenomena really to think these were the children of grandpas and grandmas that came from places like Lomza, or Wroclaw, or Rzeszow.

Well, as my grandma Kasimiera used to say about the whole thing, "rama lamma lamma ka dinga da dinga dong!"

Whatever happened to... ?

It was interesting that Jim Jacobs told us who the person he modeled Sandy Dumbrowski after, Jeanie Kozemczak. He did not indicate her status, whether *Grease* changed her life, etc. Does anyone know anything about her since those "Summer Nights" at Taft High School in Chicago?

February 2015

Lasso the moon!

Even though we live in a Jetson's world of science and technology, as you know, I remain a guy of the past. Tradition and history mean a lot to me. Along with our Polish customs, every Christmas I make a point to watch *It's a Wonderful Life*, the greatest movie ever made.

There are many angles and messages in *It's a Wonderful Life* besides the main one (which as Clarence tells George) is each "man's life touches so many other lives. When he isn't around, he leaves an awful hole." If we think our life is meaningless, worthless, or without merit, when we really examine it and think about it, we most likely have been given more and accomplished much more than we realize, and our life is important to others in ways we cannot imagine. That message is apt and worth contemplating for Americans and Polish-Americans alike.

"Wonderful Life" is the title and to prove that, the movie includes a love story, a struggle of good versus evil, human failing, human triumph, and also has touches of the ethnic for instance when Mr. Potter calls George's Savings and Loan friends "garlic eaters." But it is St. Valentine's month and so I want to dwell on the love story aspect represented in the two great romantic parts of the movie. The first is when George meets up with Mary at the dance in the high school gym and the other is when he visits her house and finally succumbs to falling in love with her.

The gym scene is reminiscent of Romeo and Juliet where George spies Mary across the room and she gazes at him. Mary's eyes light up and the two are immediately drawn to one another. They dance, laugh, and tumble into the underground pool and are "awash" in frivolity and friendship. It is a light moment, full of puppy love, and how a couple of high-school kids might act.

Sometime later, at the urging of George's mom ("nice girl that Mary; the kind that will help you find the answers George") he pays Mary a visit at her home. George Bailey is torn about where he is in life, where he is going, and what to do next; to become independent and the adventurer he yearns to be or commit to the woman he loves. Mary on the other hand is the immovable object who knows exactly what she wants and eventually captures and consumes him by her will and feminine presence that ends in one of the most passionate embraces and kisses of all time. I'm holding an ice cube on the back of my neck right now thinking about it.

An outstanding event in my wonderful world occurred most recently as a couple dear to me became engaged to be married. The young man is the son of a Polish friend who is marrying a lovely young woman, also of Polish descent. I have observed several our young people who cherish their Polish heritage frustrated about pursuing or finding someone of Polish extraction. Marriage is about a feeling of familiarity, being connected on many levels, and being comfortable around the other person. Culture and background can play a significant part of that familiarity, connectedness, and comfort so I think it is so neat that they found one another. The Polish boys and girls are out there! Hook up!

Whatever the formula in finding the "someone who will help you find the answers," whether it is dancing the Charleston, living in Bedford Falls, or simply that both of our grandmas came from Lublin, I hope and pray all our kids lasso the moon!

Happy Valentine's Day, ja cie kocham, *The Pondering Pole.*

Polish or Not?

Seen on the EthniCelebs website, Erin Brady, Miss USA 2013 is Armenian, Irish, German, and Polish. She is a Connecticut girl and does anyone from Connecticut know how Polish is she or can you find out? At a minimum, just to be in the mix of that beautiful creation, whatever the Polish percentage is noteworthy. What a gorgeous woman.

In the January Pondering Pole, I spoke about the Polish connection for the story behind the musical Grease. From Wikipedia, "One of the popular songs of the Broadway musical and 1978 movie *Grease* is 'Look at Me, I'm Sandra Dee,' in which the rebellious Rizzo satirizes new girl Sandy's (Dumbrowski) clean cut image, likened to Sandra Dee's."

The real Sandra Dee was the daughter of Mary (Cymboliak) and John Zuck who were of Carpatho-Rusyn descent. "Rusyns are an ethnic group from Eastern Europe, including Poland, where Sandra's family was from" (http://ethnicelebs.com/sandra-dee). So, a young woman from a Northwest neighborhood in Chicago was the model for Sandy Dumbrowski who was modeled after Sandra Dee, a young woman and American actress from Bayonne, New Jersey, married to the singer Bobby Darin, and whose grandparents came from Vilna and Izby Poland.

A nice tribute to Martha Stewart appeared on the *Yahoo* ticker. In a *Forbes* magazine article titled "30 Under 30 Who Are Moving the World in 2015" (http://finance.yahoo.com/news/30-under-30-moving-world-090000615.html), the actress Blake Lively, age 27 is featured as the creator of a web-site called *Preserve* that "sells clothes, food, and home goods that reflect Lively's taste in U.S.-made artisanal goods, crafts, and foods." The article mentions that "as a kid, Lively idolized Martha Stewart, and hoped to create her own lifestyle brand one day."

March 2015

Spring, at last.

*P*olish is popping up like poppies. Take your pick.

1) Janice Dickinson, model, author, and television personality. According to Wiki, she "has been described by herself and others as the first supermodel." Born in Brooklyn, New York, her Polish mother is Jennie Marie Pietrzykowski. Her book is entitled *No Lifeguard on Duty: The Accidental Life of the World's First Supermodel* (2002). Based on what I barely know of her, Janice is a good person who, despite her gifts and successes, has had a tough journey through life. I hope she is well, and I wish her peace and happiness.

2) I was surfing television stations and came upon a show called *Ridiculousness*, hosted by Rob Dyrdek. *Foxweekly* labeled Dyrdek as "one of the most influential skateboarders of all time." The special guest on that show was Polish and American model and actress Joanna Krupa and I'll tell you, the exchange between Rob and Joanna was a super cool!

   He mentioned Joanna's Polish pedigree and spoke about his own ("I'm 100% - 50% Polish" as I believe it is Rob's dad that is Polish judging by his last name). He asked Joanna about her life and career and asked her if she spoke Polish in which she replied, "Yes, I host a television show in Poland." It was a respectful and congenial conversation without any zinger to embarrass her. Nice job Rob.

3) From the Yahoo ticker, I give you the "Polish Boy" sandwich and a good but less expensive vodka.

   I was not familiar with the "Polish Boy," a super sandwich that originated and is apparently very popular in Cleveland. In a piece titled "The Best Diners in America" (https://www.yahoo.com/food/the-21-best-diners-in-america-109229674496.html), *Steve's Lunch* is on the list, a diner restaurant located in Cleveland. Here is how *Steve's* and the PB were presented in the piece.

This legendary, 24-hour diner in the Detroit-Shoreway 'hood is a 60-year institution that has seldom closed its doors since it opened them. With less than a dozen seats in the place (and tabletop jukeboxes for nostalgia), the joint does a fine breakfast, but the specialty is amazing skinless beef franks piled with dry chili (kind of like the Flint coney-style), or its take on Cleveland's own Polish Boy (piled with fries, coleslaw, and hot sauce).

You can find several references and recipes for the "Polish Boy" online and for sure, the next time I am in Cleveland I will check out *Steve's*. I'd like to hear some stories from our Cleveland readers about this diner and the "Polish Boy."

4) The other Yahoo tickler was "The Best Booze (at the Best Price) for Your Home Bar" (https://www.yahoo.com/food/this-is-how-to-build-the-best-bar-with-cheap-108834653558.html) that included the Polish vodka Luksusowa on the list. I am familiar with this brand. (Perhaps a bit too familiar with it – yikes!) My high opinion and discovery of the taste and price was echoed in a personal story. Several years back, after our meal at a local restaurant I was talking with the mixologist, and I asked him what his favorite Polish vodka was. I expected to hear Chopin or Belvedere but to my surprise, he singled out Luksusowa. There you go.

Super Bowl XLIX, Polish or Not?

On a team with a contingent of Eastern Europeans, Tom Brady, quarterback for the Super Bowl champion New England Patriots, is a quarter Polish according to EthniCelebs (http://ethnicelebs.com).

Tom's maternal grandmother was Bernice Theresa Obitz (the daughter of Charles John Obitz and Anna Stish). Bernice was of Polish descent. Charles was the son of William Obitz and Maria Ulik. Anna was the daughter of Peter Stish and Katarzyna Anastasia Koslicki.

While I was drinking Luksusowa on the rocks and watching the Super Bowl, I was also eating a couple bags of Doritos. Of course I watch the Super Bowl for the commercials and it was neat to find out that a Polish guy won the "Crash the Super Bowl" contest (http://finance.yahoo.com/news/doritos-brand-awards-one-lucky-110100151.html;_ylt=AwrBJSDTUNBUtSgAa9bQtDMD).

One lucky fan's life changed in the most incredible way today when PepsiCo's Doritos brand awarded Scott Zabielski of Los Angeles the grand prize in this year's "Crash the Super Bowl" contest – $1 million and a dream job at Universal Pictures in Hollywood. Zabielski created the best homemade Doritos ad in the ninth edition of the award-winning consumer-created ad contest, racking up the highest number of total fan votes on doritos.com.

Congrats Scott, please google "Joe Pytka," and good luck in your future film pursuits. Scott's commercial is the "Middle Seat."

April 2015

Office of the Mayor.

Popular themes of the Pondering Pole over the years have been about service and leadership. Politics is a natural combination of these two traits, and we have pondered, in one way or another, about the involvement of Polonia in this unique American governing activity.

An article about the first Polish American mayor in New England that came my way made me think about our participation in this most personal layer of the electoral relationship. I wish there was a Polish Daley or Guiliani or Cisneros and strangely there has not been one even in heavily Polish or Eastern European cities. We have dipped our toe in the water in Congress (Dingell, Mikulski, and Durenberger – mother is Cebula), as governors (Pawlenty and Kulongoski), and even with a run at the White House (Muskie).

Here are a few stories and perspectives about the Polish and "da mayor".

1) **Ben Adamowski, Chicago**. This would have been huge. Ben, the Republican, lost the 1963 election to Richard J. Daley by 11 points. According to the *Illinois Police & Sheriff's News* website (http://www.ipsn.org/characters/adam.html 1997), Ben Adamowski is shown as a very accomplished, respected, and successful man.

   Ben Adamowski was the son of Max Adamowski, a realtor in the Logan Square neighborhood and a leader in the Polish-American community for many years before his son eclipsed his accomplishments. Ben began his political odyssey as a Democrat, elected to the first of five consecutive terms in the Illinois General Assembly in 1930. At the time, the 25th senatorial district was the largest in the State...

   Adamowski came up through the ranks with the late Mayor Richard J. Daley and Federal Judge Abraham Lincoln Marovitz. Three close friends from the rough and tumble ethnic melting pot neighborhoods of Chicago: a Pole, an Irishman, and a Jew who became three of the most important and respected men in the State.

2) **Francis Slay, St. Louis**. We are lucky in St. Louis to have a mayor with a Polish connection. Francis Slay is the current and longest serving mayor in St. Louis history and whose mother is Anna Sobocinski. Over the years Francis has spoken fondly about his Polish background and has helped our community whenever possible. Suffice it to say, Francis has a warm spot in his heart for the Polish people.

The St. Louis Polish community is relatively small and the fact that Francis Slay is half Polish is just an afterthought. The real kicker for the Slay political machine in this town is his other half, the Lebanese ancestry of his father. The Lebanese in this city are engaged, involved, and very visible. There are 28 aldermen in the city and at one time four of them were of Lebanese descent. During this time Francis was President of the Board of Aldermen.

3) **Anthony J. Stonina, Chicopee, Massachusetts**. I direct you to the article in the *Masslive* website by Stephen Jendrysik that piqued my curiosity and is about the first mayor of Polish extraction elected in New England, Anthony J. Stonina (http://www.masslive.com/living/index.ssf/2015/01/stephen_jendrysik_city_hall_mob_scene_helped_usher_in_stonina_as_mayor.html).

On Jan. 4, 1932, the city of Chicopee (Massachusetts) inaugurated the city's 22nd mayor. Local officials were unprepared for the huge turnout for the Monday-morning exercises in the City Hall auditorium. In December, alderman and automobile dealer Anthony J. Stonina had defeated the incumbent mayor, Henry J. Cloutier, in a five corner contest. In spite of the closeness of the election, the region's Polish community was positively euphoric… The victory was a first for the entire six-state region.

4) **Mruk, Pankow, Kowal, and Makowski, Buffalo, New York**. Jackpot! Buffalo is a very Polish town so of course it makes sense that at least one Polonian become mayor, Mruk being the first in 1950. On the other hand, cities with large African American or Hispanic

populations have, until recently, struggled to score once if ever. Based on my astute knowledge of politics, this is very impressive and a credit to the men who won and served and the Polish coalition that supported them.

If I have missed a notable Polish American mayor of a medium or large sized city, let me know. The truth is being mayor is a tough job. Sure, there is prestige and notoriety but there is also a commitment to leadership and service. Hopefully there is at a minimum service and in most cases it is a thankless job for whatever you do, at least one person will inevitably complain.

As always, my interest is primarily, in the cases just mentioned, Poles have been part of the game. Whether we have lost but fought the good fight (Chicago), had a Polish mother to support us (St. Louis), made history with our courage and daring (Chicopee), or had practically run the board with a string of wins (Buffalo). I wish we had had more players and success in the cities with predominant Polish populations. No need to look back. I am convinced some of our young Polish men and women have the smarts and nerve to lead and serve the people, *all* the people, for the cause of humanity, and whether they realize it or not, for Polonia.

Polish or Not?

My pick for the 2014 Picture of the Year is *The Grand Budapest Hotel*. As I sat there watching the movie, I kept hearing the name of the country where the hotel was located and thought that it sure sounded familiar. "Zubrowka" is the name of the country and as we all know this is also the name of our beloved Polish bison grass vodka. That is keen and if someone knows why it was chosen to be in the story or just in the movie, let me know.

May 2015

Shout out to the polka snowbirds of Daytona.

While in Daytona Beach, Florida this past February I wandered into the Sunday polka dance at the *Polish American Pulaski Club Daytona* (http://polishamericanpulaskiclubdaytona.com). The Eddie Forman Orchestra was playing, the dancers were talented and delightful to watch, and there was a sizable group in attendance. High compliments for my dancing partner Marian who dances every dance. I was having convulsions and she barely broke a sweat. Great place, good people, and you will feel at home there. Check it out.

Readers respond.

1) Dzienkuje bardzo to jumping Joseph John Czepiel for an update on the work he is doing to have the grave of Lieutenant Matt Urban designated as notable. Please keep going on this one Joe. I feel your frustration but hang tough and be persistent as this is a cause worth pursuing. I am praying for your success.

2) Thanks also to John Skibiski for the kind words and the list of Pol-Am mayors of Massachusetts to add to those mentioned in the April Pondering Pole. MA mayors include "in Northhampton, MA was Wallace Puchalski (1961) and David Narkiewicz (2012), Holyoke, MA Daniel Szostkiewicz (1999), Walter Trybulski (1953), Robert Kumor (1971), Richard Lak (1987), and presently Richard Kos of Chicopee, MA (1997 and 2014), and in Easthampton, MA was Michael Tautznik (1996)." Go Mass!

Polish or Not?

Martha MacCallum, Fox News anchor and contributor. Born in Buffalo, New York. Her mother is Elizabeth B. MacCallum and the "B" could stand for Martha's middle name "Bowes" or perhaps it is something else. Since everyone from Buffalo is Polish, is Martha's mom, Polish or not?

I saw a super interesting thing about Dennis DeYoung, one of the key members and song writers for the rock group *Styx*. According to Wikipedia "within Styx, DeYoung acted as lead vocalist, keyboardist, *accordion player*, producer, and songwriter" (http://en.wikipedia.org/wiki/Dennis_DeYoung). Another rock star that played or incorporates the accordion. Dennis also hung with guys named Curulewski and Panozzo. Dennis DeYoung, Polish or not?

Happy Trzeciego Maja, Polish Constitution Day to all Pondering Pole and PAJ readers and subscribers.

June 2015

This is cool.

Chloe Sevigny is accomplished at a lot of things including remaining cool according to the April 22, 2015 edition of the New York Post (http://nypost.com/2015/04/22/9-reasons-why-chloe-sevigny-really-is-that-cool). The actress, designer, style icon, and now author, has a Polish mother Janine (nee' Malinowski) and was proclaimed way back in 1994 by the New Yorker magazine as "the coolest girl in the world." The Post article acknowledges that status and lists nine reasons why she "really is that cool." I believe one of the main reasons is that she has a Polish mother! Check it out as it is a fun read and a nice prop for Chloe.

Polish or Not?

Follow up to the May 2015 Pondering Pole, Dennis DeYoung of the rock group *Styx,* is not Polish, at least on his mother's side. Here is an excerpt from an article in The Huffington Post regarding Dennis' connection to the accordion (http://www.huffingtonpost.com/patricia-crisafulli/dennis-deyoung-on-the-gra_b_1656308.html):

Long before the rock band Styx broke through in the late 1970s with its showy, theatrical style, and decades before a solo career that still attracts hardcore fans of classics such as "Lady," and "Come Sail Away," there was a boy with an accordion on the south side of Chicago. Seven-year-old Dennis DeYoung heard a neighborhood kid play and, more importantly, saw how impressed his own mother was. Suddenly, young Dennis knew that this thing with bellows and buttons and shiny keys was the ticket to winning his mother's approval.

"She was Italian, and that was the law: if you're an Italian son, you must play the accordion," quipped DeYoung, who often uses humor to punctuate both life lessons and reflections on the grand illusion that is rock and roll.

First, I have never heard of the Italian fondness for the accordion although as a side note, the accordion player for the polka Mass at St. Stan's in St. Louis for many, many years was Italian. Now, can someone find out the ethnic background of Dennis' father?

Ethnicity update on Elle Macpherson who appeared on the EthniCelebs list in April as "Scottish, possibly other." Normally EC documents their findings with actual links to quotes by the person or some other verifiable reference but in this case their substantiation for her ancestry is "Elle's surname can be of Scottish origin," which is very weak proof for this website. Additionally, there is the "possibly other" part which could be 90% of her ethnicity. Pondering minds need to know, whether her birth name Gow is short for McGowen or Gowronski.

Jen Psaki, Whitehouse Communications Director is Polish and Greek according to Wikipedia (http://en.wikipedia.org/wiki/Jen_Psaki). The name Psaki reminds me of my folk dancing/singing days with the "ps" prefix prevalent in the Silesian Slask dialect. Jen is a very sharp gal who does a very good job talking around some very tough situations coming from the current Whitehouse. Keep going Jen.

Dinker's in Omaha, Nebraska is on the list, and so is Wolski's, of Wisconsin. The list is "The Most Iconic Bar in Every State (and DC)" (https://www.yahoo.com/food/the-most-iconic-bar-in-every-state-and-dc-116323911581.html). Dinker's has a Polish connection, "opened by Frank Synowiecki in 1965," but is Wolski's, Polish or not? Should be an easy one to confirm simply from the name but also from asking all the folks that have a tee-shirt that says, "I closed Wolski's." They had to be talking about something till closing!

July 2015

A family affair.

*I*nformation Technology is "it" in the United States and we lead the world in this industry. I've been watching for a Polish name in a leading or creating role connected to the Smartphone, Twitter, Facebook, and other cyber tech initiatives. Post "Woz" (Steve Wozniak of Apple), I have been disappointed not to find a readily identifiable young Polonian at the top in the current explosion in this powerful American technology sector.

Hit the jackpot for this edition of the Pondering Pole. If you did not already know it, let me introduce you to the super successful Polish woman, Susan Wojcicki, CEO of YouTube. The Wojcicki name is from her Polish-born father Stanley, the former head of the physics department at Stanford University who acquired lots of awards and recognitions.

It is probably an understatement to say that Susan Wojcicki has very good genes (mom is no slouch either) but some very successful and famous parents have duds for children. Not the case with daughter Suzanka but you can decide for yourself. This is from a *Forbes* magazine profile about her (http://www.forbes.com/profile/susan-wojcicki):

> *Memes may come and go, but Susan Wojcicki's new job is to make certain that YouTube profits from every one of them. Google employee No. 16 -- the company initially rented her Menlo Park garage as its headquarters -- now heads up the Internet's central hub for all things video. In February 2014, Wojcicki moved from her post as consigliere for Google's ads and commerce (some 90% of revenue) to become CEO of Google-owned YouTube, the world's largest video platform. It was a long time coming: In 2006, Wojcicki championed the $1.65 billion acquisition of the video site. YouTube, with more than 1 billion unique visitors a month, is now valued at some $20 billion, with 2014 revenues hitting $4 billion, up 33% from the prior year.*

Calling YouTube complementary to television, Wojcicki is working to support YouTube's celebrities and help media companies make the most of the video platform.

"Thank you for coming in Ms. Wojcicki, we'll call you… " What a resume! All that and she can dance a polka in heels. So does dad, sans heels of course, and here is a list of dad's "research interests" and career achievements from the Stanford faculty site which are quite stellar (https://physics.stanford.edu/people/faculty/stanley-wojcicki):

Research Interests

Study of neutrino oscillations using a neutrino beam created at Fermilab in Illinois and an underground detector in northern Minnesota 730 km away. The work of this group is supported by the National Science Foundation.

Career History

- **A.B., 1957, Harvard University**
- **Ph.D., 1961, University of California at Berkeley**
- **Professor of Physics, Stanford, 1974**
- **Emeritus Professor of Physics, Stanford, 2010**

Honors

- **Alfred P. Sloan Foundation Fellow, 1968-72**
- **Fellow of the American Physical Society, 1971**
- **John Simon Guggenheim Fellow, 1973-74**
- **Stanley G. Wojcicki Chair in Physics endowed, 2010**

Obviously these Wojcickis are a super smart bunch of people, and it seems that they are a very tight family. For example, I read in Wikipedia that sister Anne Wojcicki was smart to marry Google co-founder Sergey Brin and they "endowed a $2.5 million chair in experimental physics at Stanford in her father's name." That is very nice gesture in honor of the ojciec.

Polish or Not?

Walter "Walt" Woltnosz, Chairman/CEO/Co-Founder, Simulations Plus, Inc., Polish or not? Walter was instrumental in helping Stephen Hawking, the famous British theoretical physicist, cosmologist, and author cope with his debilitating medical condition by designing a "computer program called the 'Equalizer.' In a method he [Hawking] uses to this day, using a switch he selects phrases, words, or letters from a bank of about 2,500-3,000 that are scanned." (http://en.wikipedia.org/wiki/Stephen_Hawking)

Mark Zuckerberg, Chairman and CEO, Facebook, Inc. Billionaire Mark has some Polish connections in his family background. On his father and his mother's side, Mark has grandparents that emigrated from Poland (http://ethnicelebs.com/mark-zuckerberg). Check it out.

August 2015

Al's Little League.

Need to put in a plug for the Polish National Youth Baseball Foundation. For as many baseball and softball players Polish-America has produced, it is more than fitting that our European counterparts join in the fun and represent Poland in the Little League World Series. A very big dzienkuje bardzo to Al Koproski, PNYBF's National Vice President, for all the work he does on behalf of the foundation. I would encourage you to google their web site and oh, they can always use donations to help the kids. Mail them to:

Polish National Youth Baseball Foundation, C/O Al Koproski, 222 Ocean Drive East, Stamford, CT 06902-8134.

For the Polish women.

The author is Sarah Helm, *Ravensbruck, Life and Death in Hitler's Concentration Camp for Women* (Penguin Random House, LLC, 2014). Ravensbruck was unique in that it was designed to house only women and most of the prisoners were not Jewish. As Ms. Helm says in the prologue, "The facts of the Jewish genocide are today so well-known and so overwhelming that many people suppose that Hitler's extermination programme consisted of the Jewish Holocaust alone. People who ask about Ravensbruck are often surprised that the majority of the women killed there were not Jews."

Of the 130,000 women that were sent to this camp about a third of them were Polish Christians. The number of dead by starvation, execution, medical experimentation, or gassing ranges from 28,000 to 50,000. Of the number who perished, I cannot find a breakdown indicating how many were Polish.

Besides the rendering of brutality that is presented in this book and as with all the concentration camp literature, this one has a number of facets and twists that I think you will find interesting and even uplifting such as the women known as the "rabbits" and the special relationship the chief guard of Ravensbruck, Johanna Langefeld, had with the Polish prisoners.

THE PONDERING POLE 2   2020–2023 and "BEST OF"

This is a sad history, but it is also a beautiful tribute to all the women that were sent to this terrible place. They were our grandmothers, mothers, sisters, and daughters. We owe Sarah Helm bardzo gratitude for telling their story.

Polish or Not?

Pico Alexander, 24-year-old stage and film actor and writer and hottie. Born Aleksander Lukasz Jogalla, he is the son of Polish immigrants, Magdalena Deskur and Lukasz Jogalla. Check him out on ethnicelebs.com as he has a rich pedigree in the arts. We wish him well in his career in television and movies.

Jeff Glor, host of the CBS Evening News, was born in upstate New York. Polish or not?

October 2015

Son of Poland, Son of East St. Louis.

Seen in an interview on one of our local news stations was Ken Kwapis, a movie and television director who was born in East St. Louis, Illinois, and grew up in Belleville, Illinois. Both cities are across the river from St. Louis and are part of the greater metropolitan area. Wikipedia and IMDB show this home boy as being of "Polish descent."

I originally discovered Mr. Kwapis a while back when his name popped up as the director in some of *The Office* episodes. He is a busy man that Kenny Kwapis and the endeavor that brought him to the newsroom this time is his directorship of *Walk in the Woods* starring Robert Redford and Nick Nolte. One of the news anchors commented on Ken's familiarity with these two big stars as he casually remarked about "Bob" and "Nick" during the interview. Check out the lengthy list of television and movie stints for Ken Kwapis on IMDB.com. His body of work and accomplishments are quite extensive. I nominate him for a star on the St. Louis Walk of Fame.

A taste of Poland, where?

An amazing immigrant story also set in the Midwest is that of Café Poland, 807 Locust Street, Columbia, Missouri. Except for the University of Missouri, Columbia, in the middle part of the state, is just another medium to small country town, the same kind that John Mellencamp sings about. When you wonder about the feasibility of a Polish restaurant, Café Poland is a great example that proves the case and goes beyond. Determination, love, and quality of the food are the key ingredients at the root of this business plan.

Café is owned by Iwona Burlinska and her son Robert. Her other son Krystian is disabled but helps occasionally around the restaurant. The Burlinskis came to Missouri to attend Columbia College and opening the café was a way to finance it.

The family is from the northwest Polish city of Swinoujscie, near the Baltic Sea. They moved from Poland to Alaska about 10 years ago. There, Iwona ran a restaurant that was frequented by American soldiers. When they all shipped out to Iraq in 2007, she lost her business. They moved to Austin, Texas, but could not find work and could not afford the college tuition, she said. So, they moved to Columbia, where Robert will complete his degree in science in May. Iwona is working on a degree in human services.

You can read the brief story of Iwona, Robert, and Krystian in an article that appeared in the Columbia Tribune. The link is http://www.columbiatribune.com/arts_life/food/a-taste-of-poland/article_10511f1c-64c0-11e2-bc56-00127992bc8b.html.

If ever in Columbia, Missouri, stop in for a pierogi at Café Poland!

Happy Polish Heritage month, wherever you are calling home, in this country, Poland, or in some other faraway land. Wherever it is I hope you keep even a small piece of the Polish culture and memory alive in your heart or better yet on your chest.

December 2015 PAJ

Wise Children from the East.

*I*t is not often that I think about and worry for our brothers and sisters in the ancestral homeland, but there is a lot of political turmoil going on with the government and with the influx of refugees into Europe. The new president and prime minister and all the people of Poland need our thoughts and prayers as they go forward.

With that in mind, there is a small private school in St. Louis with a long and rich history doing one of the most important things in the cause of humanity and that is to teach. It is also a wonderful example of one of those rare enterprises or persons that have made it part of their mission to serve and support Polonia in a special way. Thomas Jefferson School (http://www.tjs.org/about) does just that.

Thomas Jefferson School (TJ), founded in 1946, "is an independent, non-sectarian, boarding and day school for grades 7-12." The main benefactor of TJ is philanthropist and iconoclast Charles E. Merrill, Jr., the son of Charles E. Merrill, Sr., who along with Edmund C. Lynch created the giant financial securities firm Merrill Lynch and Company.

The Polish connection comes from Charles Jr.'s "extraordinary interest in learning and cultures," a meeting and friendship with Holocaust survivor Bernat Rosner, and was bolstered by his wife Julie Boudreaux, a teacher and education innovator who established a collaboration with a similar school in Poland, Spoleczne Liceum Ogolnoksztalcace or SPLOT. "Mr. Merrill supports these efforts by sponsoring a scholarship that sends a SPLOT student to TJ each year." This scholarship has brought one student per year from Poland to TJ since 1997.

There is much more to the story than space allows, but here are two answers to a group of questions I posed to Lisa Holekamp, director of TJ about the Polish students that have attended TJ.

How has the "experiment" worked?

> *Without exception, the students who have come from TJ from SPLOT have been spectacular. They have integrated very quickly into our school community and have thrived in this setting. They have all done well academically, and have contributed a great deal to the quality of life here. Our only regret is that they can't stay longer!*

What happens to the Polish kids after they graduate? Do most stay in the U.S. or go back to Poland?

> *TJ's Polish students have traditionally returned to Poland to prepare for and take the Matura exam. Many of them have stayed in touch with TJ in the years since their stay with us.*

Polish or Not?

One of the original principles, along with Ric Ocasek, in forming the rock group *The Cars* was lead singer Benjamin Orr. Ben was born Benjamin Orzechowski in Lakewood, Ohio in 1947 and according to Wikipedia he is Polish, Russian, Czech, and German descent. The listing doesn't say what the percent of each. Benjamin Orr was the unique voice you hear in the hit song "Just What I Needed." Orr died in 2000 of pancreatic cancer. What percent Polish is the Slavic looking rocker Benjamin "Orzechowski" Orr?

Into Dancing with the Stars are you? Into dancing swing? I have a treat for you. Check out the name Michael Kielbasa on YouTube. A West Coast guy and a West Coast Swing (a style of dancing) guy, you can read this brief summary of his dancing life (http://www.michaelkielbasa.com):

Michael has been training and dancing for the past 20 years, in most styles of Partner Dancing. He lives in San Diego, California and teaches out of Starlight Dance Studio. As one of the top Champion West Coast Swing Professionals Michael has been traveling, teaching and performing not only in the United States but in countries like Canada, France, Germany, Russia, United Kingdom, Brazil and Australia.

What a hoofer!! Is Michael a "kiolbasa" or some other kind of sausage? Polish or not?

Wesolych Swiat to the Journal readers and blessings and peace to our Polonian bretheren here and around the world. We have so much to be thankful for.

IX
Dziekuje Bardzo!

Dziekuje Bardzo

Dziekuje bardzo (pronunciation: jane-koo'-yeah bard'-zoe) in Polish means "thank you very much" and at the end of some Pondering Pole columns I acknowledge and thank people that provided leads or information that was useful and worth noting in the writing of the column.

I am listing those from 2020-2023 and those from "Best of" for the most part in their original form and if I missed you forgive me for the oversight, but I am grateful you participated.

Besides those contributing with the articles, I also thank my family and the Saint Louis Polish community for their support and feedback for this version of the Pondering Pole. A big thank you to Mike Koziatek, reporter for the Belleville News-Democrat (in Illinois) for reading through the columns, suggesting edits, and giving me his opinions. I want to thank Graphic Connections and Kim Koenig for their work in putting the book together. Thanks again, especially to my wife Sue. As before, she often prodded to keep me on track, and gave me great encouragement by honestly assessing and enjoying what I wrote. That meant a lot.

As before, two people need special recognition. The first is the editor of the Polish American Journal Mark Kohan for giving me the opportunity to fulfill my quest to reveal Polish connections and excite the folks (hopefully) with thought-provoking ideas and information. The other is Jack Jackowski, a Polish American Journal reader from Michigan and my number one researcher supplying me with leads and confirmation on important and successful Polish people, places, and events. I consider him an associate, collaborator, and a good friend.

Here is the list of dziekuje bardzos from 2020 through 2023 and "Best of."

January 2020 - A big dziekuje bardzo to Jack Jackowski for the many leads provided in the last month and really, throughout 2019. He knows, as I do, there is an entire world out there of interesting people, places, and events that have a Polish connection, and it is refreshing to hear his thoughts. Though this is a little late, Wesoly Swiat to you and your family no matter what nation or land you reside or as we know from the Christmas story, where you journey to be included in the census.

THE PONDERING POLE 2   2020–2023 and "BEST OF"

September 2020 - I owe a bunch of dziekuje bardzos (thank you very much) for this month's Pondering Pole. Thank you, Mark Kohan for telling me about Mike Yurosek and his idea for Whole Baby Carrots. Thank you to Jeffrey Lesser for the nice email and information on his uncle Leonard "the legend" Soloway. Thank you again, Officer Cameron Maciejewski for saving that baby's life.

November 2020 - Dziekuja bardzo to Susan Gromacki Lathrop for pointing me to Jarrett Krosoczka. With grandkids I can always use another children's book to give away. Happy Thanksgiving to all the Pondering Pole and PAJ readers.

December 2020 - Dziekuje bardzo to Jarek Czernikiewicz for his favorite Warsaw neighborhood picks.

January 2021 - New year, new adventures, and hopefully both will be COVID free. Stay safe. Dziekuje bardzo to Mark Kohan for the tip on Marcin Dorocinski.

March 2021 - Received a nice letter from Walter Piatek. Thank you for the information on your family and St. Joseph's Church Walter. I enjoyed hearing from you and thank you for being a dedicated Polish American Journal reader and supporter. Thanks also to Jack Jackowski for the lead.

May-June 2021 - Dziekuje bardzo to Jack Jackowski for the information on *Cocktails with a Curator* and *The Polish Rider*. Loved it though I need to buy another bottle of Zubrowka.

July-August 2021 - Dziekuje bardzo to Irena Szewiola for the kind words and the strong Polish spirit. DB as well to my daughter Alina (graduate USC Film School) for the alert on Liz Kloczkowski's nomination.

April 2022 - Does not happen often, but I received three responses to Pondering Pole columns. An authentic dziekuje bardzo to the Susans: Dr. Susan Gromacki Lathrop, Ms. Susan Rydzewski, and Susan Yost regarding thoughts about the *Clarinet Polka* book, memories of Lodz, and why it is okay to "have fun and laugh a little." Big, big thanks also to Jack Jackowski for the confirmation on Stephen Rusckowski's ancestral background. Wesolego Alleluja and have fun and laugh a little for Easter.

Dziekuje Bardzo

May-June 2022 - Thank you, as always, to my number one spotter for all things Polish, Jack Jackowski for his interest and help with this month's Pondering Pole. Thank you also to Mark Kohan for your support, and to Paula for her Oscypek experience. Have a Happy Constitution Day.

July-August 2022 - Thanks to Ronald Rychlak for information pertaining to members of the board for the Catholic League and news about the *MAUS* initiative. Dziekuje to Alice and Tony Kaminski for sharing their wonderful family with us. I want to be in their family.

September 2022 - Dziekuje bardzo to Mark Kohan for sending the YouTube link about the lovely Sara James.

November 2022 - Dziekuje bardzo to Paula from Toledo for the link to the *Soul of Christ* music. Thank you also, Jeff Piotrowski, for the engaging conversation and real-life stories of extreme weather tracking. Everyone have a great Thanksgiving, and considering Ian, count your blessings and know you have much to be thankful for.

January 2023 - A big dziekuje bardzo to my daughter Alina for pointing me to David Baszucki. It was an obvious one though as her son, my grandson Lucca, is a fan of Roblox.

March 2023 - Big dziekuje bardzo to Jack Jackowski for tracing Terry Pegula's roots. The cold case is finally solved. Thanks also to Mark Kohan for pointing me to Chris Dreja. One was a long-held suspicion realized and the other enlightened me about rock history that I was unaware of. Finally, thank you Roger Moorhouse for writing such an important book, *Poland 1939*. Happy Pulaski Day!

April 2023 - Dziekuje bardzo to Tony Murawski for getting me thinking about Polish sauerkraut and to Cousin Jody for Grandma Rose's recipe. Thank you again Father Joncas for all you have done for God's people and the Church. Wesolego Alleluja to all the Pondering Poles and subscribers of the Polish American Journal. Hope you have blessed and joyful Easter and be sure to enhance your meal with ample amounts of Twarog and Polish sauerkraut.

Best Of

August 2013 - A duzy dziekuje bardzo to Ed Drobinski for the tale about his family that eats together and stays together. Also, ddb to Raymond Cwieka for sending me the papers and videos on Polish dance. Very interesting and educational and I am enjoying the material.

September 2013 - Dziekuje bardzo to Joseph Czepiel for the information and questions regarding Tadeusz Kosciuszko and his nationality. You got me pondering.

October 2014 - Dziekuje bardzo to Mark Kohan and Larry Trojak for the lead about Karol Lapinski. I feel like I know this man very well and am so happy we are part of the same ancestral family.

November 2014 - Dziekuje bardzo to Jack Jackowski for the lead on Lyda Roberti. Said Jack, "Check out Lyda Roberti, Warsaw born, Broadway & Hollywood star who tragically died at age 31 (1906 - 1938). YouTube has 3 clips of her singing with her comedic Polish accent. She has a magnetic personality and looks like a Polish Jean Harlow. Too bad she died at her blossoming career." Fun and interesting gal. Please check her out.

Dziekuje bardzo also to all the Lucerne County, Pennsylvanians that contacted me affirming that Polonia is very alive and well in this part of the country. About half the county eMailed me so yes, this is a predominantly Polish land. To Debbie, John, Ray, Sharon, and JC, Na Zdrowie! and God bless and keep up the great spirit that I know you have!!

January 2015 - Dzienkuje Bardzo to Tony Kaminski and the Polish Polka program for the "Very Important Polish Person" award to the Pondering Pole. This means a lot to me, already framed and hanging it on my wall, and I really appreciate it.

February 2015 - Dzienkuje Bardzo to Joseph John Czepiel for the holiday greetings and interesting information especially about the Mummer's New Year's Eve parade in Philadelphia. Never knew it existed, the history of it, the spectacle of it all, and so thank you Joseph for that. Check out the Polish American String Band *50 Shades of Hay* on the official Mummer's Parade website http://mummers.com for 2015. I was very impressed with the group's performance, and you can watch it yourself from the website.

Dziekuje Bardzo

March 2015 - Good to hear from Ron Tomczik regarding the Polish Enigma code breakers. Your eMail piqued my interest Ron so much that I have been doing some research. The Polish involvement is an interesting study, and I would encourage all Polonians to become familiar with this part of World War II. You can judge for yourself the degree of significance of the Polish contribution.

April 2015 - Dzienkuje Bardzo to Don Binkowski for the eMails on a whole host of Polish topics. I enjoy reading them Don and keep it coming. Wesolego Alleluja and Happy Easter to all the PAJ readers and subscribers.

July 2015 - Dzienkuje bardzo to Tom Tarapacki for the tip about the Wojcickis and Walter Woltnosz. Thank you, Larry Trojak, for "tidbit" on the Polish connections for the cartoon and character *Dora the Explorer*.

September 2015 - Dzienkuje bardzo to Dick Kozacko for the inquiry on Jeff Glor. Enjoy the rest of the summer and have a tomato for me.

December 2015 - Dzienkuje bardzo to Mark Kohan for the lead on Ben Orr, and dzienkuje bardzo to Charles Merrill Jr. and all the teachers and staff at Thomas Jefferson School for giving a Polish kid an excellent education and unique cultural experience.

After reading *The Pondering Pole 2*, if you have a thought about any topic presented, have a question, or have interesting facts to share, eMail me at alinabrig@yahoo.com.

N.B. If you send eMail, reference the *Polish American Journal* or *The Pondering Pole* in the subject line. I will not open an eMail if I do not recognize the subject or the sender.